CONTENTS

*Finding
Them,
Keeping
Them*

FINDING THEM, KEEPING THEM:

Effective Strategies for Evangelism and Assimilation in the Local Church

Gary McIntosh & Glen Martin

B&H PUBLISHING GROUP

Nashville, Tennessee

© Copyright 1992 B & H Publishing Group
All rights reserved
Printed in the United States of America

13-digit ISBN: 978-0-8054-6051-3
10-digit ISBN: 0-8054-6051-9

Dewey Decimal Classification: 254.5
Subject Heading: CHURCH MEMBERSHIP
Library of Congress Card Catalog Number: 91-20168

Unless otherwise noted, all Scripture quotations are from the New American Standard Bible. © The Lockman Foundation, 1960, 1962, 1963, 1968, 1971, 1972, 1973, 1975, 1977. Used by permission.

Library of Congress Cataloging-in-Publication Data

McIntosh, Gary, 1947–
    Finding them, keeping them / Gary McIntosh and Glen Martin
        p.   cm.
    ISBN: 0-8054-6051-9
    1. Church growth. 2. Evangelistic work. 3. Church membership.
    I. Martin, Glen, 1953–   II. Title.
    BV652.25.M318   1992
    254´.5—dc20   91-20168
                                                            CIP

12 13 14 15 16 17 18 19 20   10 09 08 07 06

Preface

People are looking! Looking for God, looking for supportive relationships with others who love and care for them. That is the thrust of this book: finding those who are looking for God and keeping those who are looking for relationships.

Gary's parents haven't been to church in forty years. They grew up in Oklahoma and attended their small Baptist church every time the doors were open. When a fire destroyed their home, they moved to Colorado. After establishing a new residence, they began looking for a new church. However, their "Okie" mannerisms were not acceptable to the churches they visited. After several tries, they gave up, never to be involved on a regular basis in church again. They were looking for a relationship, but no church seemed interested in keeping them.

My own father died two years ago. He was a great man, a man who was morally strong and ethically sound. He was a good provider and a caring father. How grateful I was that, despite my efforts and failures, God answered my prayers for his salvation after a dear associate of mine shared the simplicity of the gospel with him. He had been a Christian for only a year before cancer began to take his life from him.

As I sat by his bedside, he shared with his shallow breath, "Son, God's waiting for me, I'll be waiting for you." I look back on that precious thought with both tears and a burden. There are many other men and women, boys and girls, for whom God is waiting in glory, yet they need to be found by Christians who are willing to share their faith.

My burden does not end with *finding them,* however. When people experience new life in Christ, the church has an obligation to incorporate them into its fold. The church has the responsibility to train and equip these individuals in the process of sanctification so that they will experience the fulfillment that Christ so wants us to enjoy.

Can we *find* these people and, once they receive Christ, *keep* them in the church? Yes! As Gary and I have worked in local churches for many years, and consulted with groups, churches, and denominations, we have put together a methodology and a strategy for finding and keeping new Christians that has proven to be effective and well received. This book is the fruit of hours of listening to struggling pastors, and years of seeing people come and go.

Can your church grow? Yes! God's richest blessings await the leadership that evaluates and plans effective strategies for church growth.

Introduction
Have You Ever Seen a Pigeon Walking?

Have you ever wondered why a pigeon walks so funny? According to an interesting article in the *Detroit Free Press,* a pigeon walks the way it does so it can see where it's going. Since a pigeon can't adjust its focus as it moves, it actually has to bring its head to a complete stop between steps in order to refocus. This is the way it walks: head forward, stop; head back, stop. Don't laugh—that's how it goes!

As church leaders, we often have the same problem as the pigeon—we have a hard time seeing while we're moving. We need to stop between steps to refocus on where we are in relation to the world and the will of God.

How Do Churches Grow?

In simple terms, there are only two ways to grow a church: we must bring people in the "front door," and we must keep people from going out the "back door."

The front door is the way people come into a church. Traffic flows through the front door in three ways. One way is what we call "biological growth." This form of growth is merely the children of church members growing up, receiving Christ, and joining a church. In North America biological growth normally equals 2.5 percent of a church's worship attendance. Another way people come into a church is through "transfer." As people move, face job relocation, or become disheartened with their current church, they transfer membership. Transfer growth represents 8 percent of a church's worship attendance. The third way people flow into a church is through "conversion." As people hear the gospel and respond in personal faith, they need a church home. Conversion growth normally equals 5 percent of a church's worship attendance (see fig. 1).

For example, during one year a church with two hundred in worship attendance will likely see five people join through "biological" growth, sixteen people through "transfer" growth, and ten people through "conversion" growth, for a total of thirty-one people. These three paths into a church are always open, but there are also ways out of a church.

The "back door" is the way people leave a church. Traffic flows out of a church's back door in three ways. The first way is through death. Each year many of God's saints are called home to be with the Lord. A church typically loses to death 1 to 2 percent of its total worship attendance each year. A second way people leave a church is through "transfer." As people transfer into one church, they are also transferring out of another. In general, a church loses 2 to 3 percent of its worship attendance through this means. A third way out is through "reversion." People slowly drift away from a church without uniting with another one. In North America "reversion" accounts for 2 to 6 percent of a church's losses in worship attendance (see fig. 2).

For example, a church with two hundred in worship attendance will likely lose four people through death, six people through "transfer," and up to twelve people through "reversion," for a total of twenty-two.

In order to find them and keep them, we need to stop, refocus our direction, then move ahead. Having spent

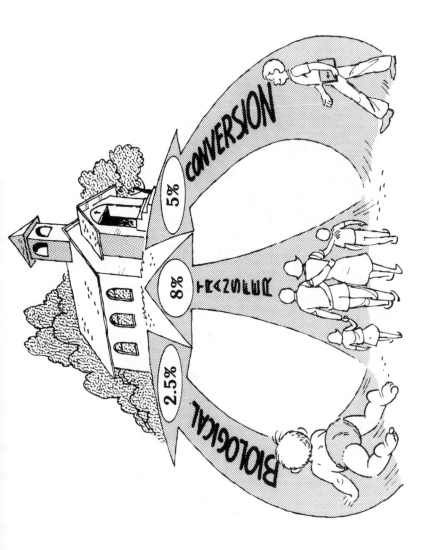

Figure 1

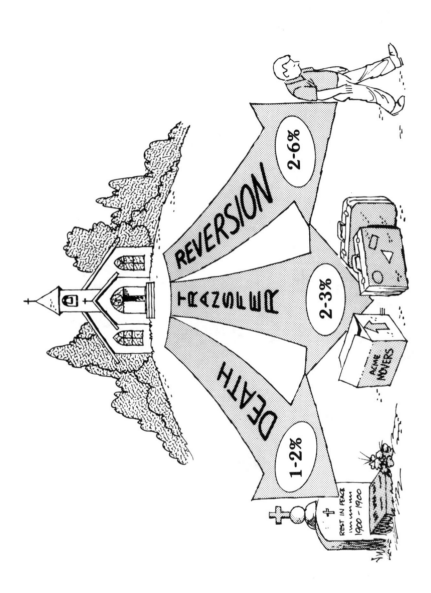

many hours working in local churches, evaluating their strengths and their weaknesses, I have come to the conclusion that there are two key questions upon which we must focus.

Question #1: How can we develop strategies that will bring more people in our front door?

Question #2: How can we develop strategies that will keep people from leaving through our back door?

This book focuses on ten strategies. Five strategies will answer the first question and enable a church to reach new people for Christ. The other five strategies will answer the second question and enable a church to assimilate new members.

Five Strategies for Finding Them

Casey Stengel once said, "It's easy to get good players. Gettin' em to play together, that's the hard part." What is true in baseball is also true in the ministry of the local church. At least five key players or strategies must be united and balanced in a local church to achieve effective evangelism.

Evangelism Strategy 1: Be Present in Your Community

The Salvation Army has made it clear that they want to be present in times of crisis. They want to be the extension of the loving Savior's hand into the community. They are an army that has taken to heart the words of Christ when He said, "For I was hungry, and you gave Me something to eat; I was thirsty, and you gave Me drink; I was a stranger, and you invited me in; naked, and you clothed Me; I was sick, and you visited Me; I was in prison, and you came to Me" (Matt. 25:35-36). Like the Salvation Army, a local church must be willing to establish a presence in its community. Church leaders must answer the question, "Who are we helping?"

Evangelism Strategy 2: Proclaim the Gospel

Campus Crusade for Christ's burden is proclaiming Christ. Dr. Bill Bright's focus, passed down to his staff, is vividly portrayed in the way he signs his letters: "Yours for fulfilling the Great Commission in this generation, Bill." Like Campus Crusade for Christ, a local church must have effective ways to communicate the gospel to lost people. Church leaders must answer the question, "How are we helping people to hear the good news?"

Evangelism Strategy 3: Persuade People to Accept Christ

Billy Graham focuses on another form of reaching our world—persuasion. His life has been dedicated to sharing the news of salvation with millions of people and creating within his listeners the desire to respond. His ministry is similar to that of the apostle Paul, who knew the fear of the Lord and persuaded people. Like Billy Graham, a local church must have effective ways to help people accept Christ. Church leaders must answer the question, "How are we helping people make decisions for Christ?"

Evangelism Strategy 4: Help People Progress in the Christian Life

The Navigators have helped us see the need for discipleship, or what we call "progression evangelism."

> You can lead a soul to Christ in from 20 minutes to a couple of hours, but it takes from 20 weeks to a

couple of years to get him on the road to maturity, victorious over the sins and recurring problems that come along."[1]

Navigators have the progression of the saint as their dream. They see the call to "make disciples" as their scriptural focus, and have designed follow-up programs and materials to accomplish just that. Like the Navigators, a local church must have effective ways to disciple new converts. Church leaders must answer the question, "How are we helping people continue in their faith?"

Evangelism Strategy 5: Help People Produce New Believers

All of these ingredients are vital to the growth of a church, and this fifth ingredient is necessary to balance our evangelistic strategy. We call it "production evangelism." This component of evangelism takes to heart the need to train church members so that they become witnesses for Christ. We must answer, "How are we helping people learn to share their faith?"

Chapters 1 through 5 of this book focus on this issue of balancing evangelism. Each chapter allows you to evaluate your church in each crucial area. Next, an evaluation chapter helps you develop a balanced strategy of evangelism in your church.

Five Strategies for Keeping Them

Just as people enter the church and become responsible members, others walk out of the "back door" disillusioned or hurt. When an equal number of people are coming in and going out, the church appears to be growing when it has actually plateaued.

Like the five strategies for balanced evangelism, there are also five strategies which enable a church to have an effective assimilation strategy.

Assimilation Strategy 1: Help People Develop Friendships

While I was on a tour of the giant California sequoias, a guide pointed to one of these great trees and mentioned that it has roots that grow barely below the surface. Sequoia trees only grow in groves, and their roots intertwine under the surface of the earth. When the strong winds come, they hold each other up. In a sense, people are like the giant sequoias. Family, friends, neighbors, the church body, and other groups are reinforcing. When the strong winds of life blow, these people serve as reinforcement to hold each other up. Church leaders must answer the question, "How are we helping our people develop friendships?"

Assimilation Strategy 2: Help People Become Involved

Everyone yearns to feel secure and significant. While friendships provide security, appropriate responsibility provides a sense of significance. New people want to be valued for their contribution as well as loved. Effective assimilation occurs only when people take on a specific position, designated function, or a new responsibility. People who feel good about the contributions they are making are less likely to drop out. Church leaders must answer the question, "How are we helping our people to use their gifts and talents?"

Assimilation Strategy 3: Help People Belong

In the early church, the quality of the Christians' relationships in the group setting was the measure of their

Christian authenticity. Scripture records that the first disciples met in large groups for public worship and in small groups for fellowship. It was in the small groups that people found a strong sense of bonding that resulted in effective ministry. Relating to small groups, as well as to large crowds, was the key to communicating the gospel and generating enthusiasm. Church leaders must answer the question, "How are we helping our people find a place to belong?"

Assimilation Strategy 4: Help People Work Together

Good group morale is an elusive goal. Effective assimilation takes place when the church learns how to get people to work together and for each other. Not only does good *esprit de corps* enable people to get more accomplished in less time, it also draws in new people. Since many visitors and new members find it difficult to identify with the vision, leadership, or values of a church, leaders must develop a plan of orientation that will create ownership in a church's ministry. They must answer the question, "How are we helping our people identify with our values and goals?"

Assimilation Strategy 5: Help People Grow in Their Faith

Living in Southern California gives us opportunity to drive to the beach and take an occasional reflective stroll along the shore. When there has been a storm out in the Pacific and the winds are up, I most enjoy watching the sea gulls gracefully riding the currents as they flee turbulent weather offshore. Many of the people in our churches are fleeing storms. They are looking for currents of grace that will both lift them up and cause them to move forward once again. Church leaders must answer the question, "How are we helping our people face the realities of life?"

How does your church measure up? Chapters 6 through 10 will focus on this issue of balancing assimilation. Each of these chapters will help you evaluate your own church in one crucial area. Last, an evaluation chapter will provide a way to help you develop a balanced strategy of assimilation in your church.

So, have you ever seen a pigeon walking? Let's begin walking like pigeons as we examine our own churches and plan effective strategies to find new people and keep them. Are you ready? Head forward, stop; head back, stop. Don't laugh—that's how it goes!

Note

[1]Dawson Trotman, *Born to Reproduce* (Colorado Springs: Nav Press, 1986), 30.

Part 1
*Finding
Them:
Evangelism*

1
Presence Evangelism

Through the quiet streets of a fishing village that lay at the mouth of the turbulent river, a cry rang out, "Boy overboard!" Quickly a crowd gathered, and anxious eyes looked out over the rushing water to the figure of the drowning boy. Each anxious mother's heart was asking, "Is he my boy?" A rope was brought and the strongest swimmer in the village volunteered to rescue the drowning lad. Tying one end of the rope to his waist, he threw the other among the crowd and plunged in. Anxiously, they watched him breast the tide with strong, sure strokes, and a cheer went up when he reached the boy and grasped him safely in his powerful arms. "Pull in the rope!" he shouted over the swirling waters. The villagers looked from one to another, "Who is holding the rope?" they asked. But no one was holding the rope! In the excitement of watching the rescue, the end of the rope had slipped into the water. Powerless to help, they watched two precious lives go down because no one had made it his business to hold the rope.

This story illustrates the essentials of an effective evangelism strategy in a local church. First, the villagers were aware of the needs of the drowning boy. Someone must have been monitoring the river looking for people in trouble. When they spotted the boy, they alerted the village.

Second, the villagers were willing to jump into the water to help the drowning boy. They didn't stand on the shore, yelling at the boy to let him know he was drowning. They sent one of their own people into the waters, even at great risk, to rescue the boy.

Third, the villagers were pulling the boy to safety. Of course, in the story they forgot to hold the rope, but the strategy was sound.

In the Sermon on the Mount, Jesus revealed some of His thoughts about presence evangelism. He said we are like salt: present, yet invisible; unseen by the naked eye, but very noticeable by taste. He also described our influence as light in the darkness. Obvious to the sight, the light can be seen easily.

Churches that are effectively reaching people for Christ see the needs of the unchurched, establish ministries that allow the church to be present in the community, and have a process by which they are able to draw these unchurched people into the safety of Christ and a local church.

The church today is often not adjusting itself to what is going on around it. Quite often statements like, "What difference does it make?" are heard ringing through the halls of government and education. This comes in a time of resignation and bewilderment. We cannot allow ourselves the luxury of indifference. We must be positive agents of change. God in Christ made a difference! God in Noah made a difference! God in the early churches made a difference! And God in us and God through the churches of today can make a difference!

This difference, however, is not measured by pious pronouncements from pulpits but by living a life-style committed to the Lord Jesus. Many people look at the church and see it as a major stumbling block. They say "Yes" to God and "No" to the church. Why didn't the early church suffer with this apathy? Looking at their united testimony, one soon realizes that their mutual interaction and caring attitude showed genuine Christian love, and there will never be anything more attractive than that. The early church wasn't stagnant. The early church wasn't dull. *It was on fire!* It made its presence felt in its community in three ways.

First, it was present in the normal network of society. The twelve disciples are a prime example. They were men who lived and worked in the normal social structure of their time. Peter, James, and John were fishermen. Matthew was a tax collector. Simon was a countercultural rebel. When these and the rest of the disciples came to Christ, they didn't leave their social network of family, friends, and associates. They remained in those natural, social structures as living witnesses to Christ's power.

Remember Matthew? What did he do after receiving Christ as his Savior? Did he quit his work and go to seminary? No! We are told in Luke 5:29 that he "made him a great feast in his own house: and there was a great company of [tax collectors] and of others that sat down with them" (KJV). Who is "them"? Matthew and Jesus! God expects believers to maintain presence in the natural, social network of society so that they have a direct witness to unbelievers. In this way the unbeliever sees that our lives are different.

As I look at my own life, I can clearly see times when I was a strong witness for Christ and when I was not. In every instance of strong witness, I was employed in secular work. I was around non-Christians much of the time. My witness was most effective because local church evangelism begins with its people living, working, and playing with non-Christians. Maintaining a presence in the community is vital.

Second, they were present in ministry to the physical needs of people.

> Now at this time some prophets came down from Jerusalem to Antioch. And one of them named Agabus stood up and began to indicate by the Spirit that there would certainly be a great famine all over the world. And this took place in the reign of Claudius. And in the proportion that any of the disciples had means, each of them determined to send a contribution for the relief of the brethren living in Judea. And this they did, sending it in charge of Barnabas and Saul to the elders (Acts 11:27-30).

Agabus comes into Antioch and relates to them that a famine is soon to come upon the people in Jerusalem. Now granted, we could spend a lot of time studying the causes and effects of their needs in the holy city, but let's focus on the desire to be present by the leadership in Antioch. Did the leadership say, "Well, . . . their theology is not the same as ours so let's stay clear"? Was a letter written to those abiding in Jerusalem saying, "We pray that this will prove to be a lesson in good financial management"? No! They saw a need and desired to be present to meet that need. This type of ministry is not new. Churches have always responded to such needs. All of us are familiar with the work of the Salvation Army, Goodwill, the YMCA, and YWCA.

It is this kind of practical, presence-caring which makes such an impact on the receptibility of the gospel. This is why so many mission boards now commission tent-maker missionaries to go into distant lands to meet a need, demonstrate their faith, then establish a church. The fastest growing ministries are ones which speak directly to felt needs. Churches are finding that ministries such as divorce recovery, single parenting, and dealing with substance abuse are well attended. This is presence evangelism. It is a major part of establishing a complete evangelism strategy in a local church.

Third, the early Christians were present in the spiritual battle for people's souls. They decided that they needed to have their presence felt beyond the walls of their church homes and city protection. They commissioned Paul and Barnabas to go on their first missionary endeavor to extend their personal presence beyond what the church could reach. Two of the greatest men in this church were released for God's work because this church cared, and it is this kind of church that not only wins souls, but also holds those new converts.

Understanding the Process of Evangelism

Viewing local church evangelism as a funnel may be helpful. The large top is open to receive as many unchurched people as possible so that disciples are made through the process of time, resulting in full grown disciples at the bottom (see fig. 3).

In the process of evangelism, an individual moves through several stages as an observer, a hearer, a learner, a believer, a worker, and a discipler. Adding this to our first model, we can see the evangelism process develop (fig. 4).

Presence evangelism is the large open end of the funnel where unchurched people are initially contacted through need-meeting ministries so that they may sense the warmth and acceptance of Christianity. This is an environment free of the pressures to conform and immediately align themselves with the group's identity.

Developing Your Strategy

In planning an effective evangelism strategy, your church will need to establish its presence among un-

Figure 3

AN ONLOOKER

A HEARER

A BELIEVER

A LEARNER

A DISCIPLER

PRESENCE EVANGELISM

MINISTRIES
IN PLACE
1. _____
2. _____
3. _____

MINISTRIES
NEEDED
1. _____
2. _____
3. _____

EVANGELISM

Figure 4

churched people through several need-meeting ministries. As a rule of thumb, you should be able to identify a minimum of three ministries which establish a presence among the unchurched. For example, I've worked with churches who have hosted a cake-decorating class. Another church offered a tole painting class in the evening. Many churches offer sports programs, such as volleyball and softball, to make contact with the unchurched.

At this point you need to make a list of all of your church ministries. List every ministry you are able to think of at this time. Do so below.

All the Ministries of My Church

Now that you have completed a listing of your church ministries, look over the list and underline those which establish a presence in the unchurched community. To help you think this through, consider the following. Underline those ministries which

- Are strictly for unchurched people
- Have a nonchurch atmosphere

- Are nonthreatening to unchurched people
- Have at least 50 percent of the people in attendance unchurched

List the underlined ministries below.

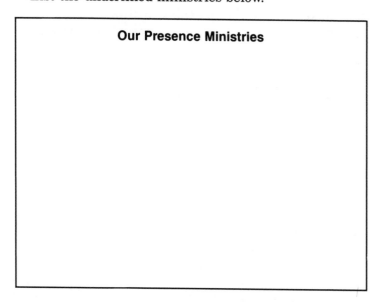

Our Presence Ministries

Do you have at least three presence ministries? If not then you will need to develop additional ministries that touch the lives of the unchurched. Transfer your presence ministries to figure 4 and identify the number of presence ministries still needed.

Summary

A certain South African missionary society once wrote to David Livingstone: "Have you found a good road to where you are? We want to know how to send some men to join you." Livingstone wrote back: "If you have men who will come only if they know there is a good road, I don't want them. I want men who will come if there is no road."

Holding the rope in our community often means going into areas that have no roads, no obvious entry points. Nowhere in the Bible do we read, "Bring them to church and make disciples." God's call has always been to meet the people where they are, to be present with them.

2
Proclamation Evangelism

Our age of technology has placed a major emphasis on high I.Q.'s Here is an I.Q. test for you. No, it's not the Intelligence Quotient that we are interested in. This is an interesting test about something much more important to the church and much more evident—your *Invitation Quotient*. Take the test and see how you rate. Circle YES or NO at the right.

1. Have you spoken to anyone in the last month to share with them what Jesus Christ and His church mean to you?   YES   NO

2. Did you speak to someone in the last month who has been absent from the services to express your concern for them?   YES   NO

3. Have you invited a newcomer to the community to come with you to church any time in the past four months?   YES   NO

4. Have you encouraged or invited anyone who does not attend any Sunday School or church to visit yours with you in the last month?   YES   NO

5. Did you speak to someone last Sunday you did not know personally who was in the church services to extend your personal word of greeting and welcome?   YES   NO

6. Have you taken time to greet the people who sit next to you in the pew before or after the church services? YES NO

7. Do you pray for opportunities to be able to speak about Christ or your church to others? YES NO

8. Do you pray that the Holy Spirit will burden you with the souls of the lost people around you? YES NO

Now, that wasn't too hard, was it? Now that you have taken our little quiz, how did you score? If you got eight "YES" answers, your I.Q. is terrific. Five "YES" answers rate you in the category of a "cold fish." And with only three or fewer "YES" answers, please stop reading, and take your pulse.

Now don't worry if your score was low, there is hope. Every church with a renewed vision can revitalize their *Invitation Quotient.*

There are people around you every day who are waiting for someone to care enough about them to offer a warm, genuine invitation to the fellowship of your church. Recent studies have found that one-fourth of all unchurched people say they have never been invited to church but would come if they were invited.[1] They long to have someone proclaim to them that he is excited about his Christian faith and equally as enthusiastic about his church. Churches made up of Christians who are present in the lives of non-Christians will learn to proclaim the good news.

Of course, giving an invitation at an event is just the first step. Eventually, proclamation must center on explanation of the life, death, and resurrection of Jesus Christ and personal commitment. Yet many churches find the entire scope of proclamation an endless struggle. From simple invitation to church services to sharing the explicit steps to salvation, most churches are ineffec-tive. There are two main reasons for this ineffectiveness.

First, most churches have frankly lost touch with the unchurched. Jesus was always at home with sinners and they with Him.

> And He went out again by the seashore; and all the multitude were coming to Him, and He was teach-ing them. And as He passed by, He saw Levi the son of Alphaeus sitting in the tax office, and He said to him, "Follow Me!" And he rose and followed Him. And it came about that He was reclining at the table in his house, and many tax-gatherers and sinners were dining with Jesus and His dis-ciples; for there were many of them, and they were following Him. And when the scribes of the Phar-isees saw that He was eating with the sinners and tax-gatherers, they began saying to His disciples, "Why is He eating and drinking with tax-gatherers and sinners?" (Mark 2:13-17)

Jesus never would have impacted their lives if He had not known how to relate to their lives. He never majored on the minors, insisting on "appropriate dress," or man-dating a "high-church" vocabulary. Jesus was "all things to all people."

For example, consider the proclamation of God's Word during any church service. When visitors and new Chris-tians enter the arena of your worship services, are they intimidated by the liturgy? Do they feel inadequate and lost in trying to follow the words of a hymn or song? After all, what is an Ebenezer, and how do I raise mine? Be aware that not everyone in your services will know the Lord's Prayer or the Doxology by memory; thus, we must examine our services through the eyes of the yet unlearned.

Second, most churches confuse being a *witness* with

being an *evangelist*. Acts 1:8 clearly tells us that everyone is to be a witness to the good that God has done in his or her life. There are no exceptions to the mandate to do this kind of work. Most of us begin with a thousand excuses. We are too scared, too young, too old, too busy—then we find that what we mean is that we are too lazy, too selfish, too self-indulgent, too set in our ways. The real truth is that the depth of an experience of Christ may be measured by our inability to keep still about it. When people find Christ fully, they have and will continue to have a message about Him for those with whom they come in contact.

There is a woman in our church named Dorothy Swoverland, a dear saint and the wife for forty-five years of a now retired pastor. Early in the 1980s, when Marshall, her husband, was still in the ministry full time, her doctors discovered she had cancer. Dorothy went through an extensive time of surgery and chemotherapy, yet her life still demonstrated the fullness found only in Jesus Christ. She would pray through the church directory between the nausea and emesis; she wrote letters of encouragement to the ill and struggling in her church; while on a gurney on the way to surgery, she even experienced the joy of leading a nurse to Christ. Today, she stands as a pillar to all Christians in our church, a living testimony to the call to "make disciples" despite our excuses.

However, not all are called to be evangelists. While there is no clear Scripture passage to prove this point, there are a number of inferences. Ephesians 4:11 states that Christ has given "some as apostles, and some as prophets, and some as evangelists, and some as pastors and teachers." Logically, while not everyone is a pastor, so not all are evangelists. Note also Acts 21:8, "And on the next day we departed and came to Caesarea; and entering the house of Philip the evangelist, who was one of the seven, we stayed with him." Philip is expressly called an evangelist. He was much more effective in bringing people to Christ than were the other six appointed in Acts 6. He had specific giftedness to proclaim the gospel. Paul wrote to Timothy, "do the work of an evangelist" (2 Tim. 4:5). Apparently, Timothy was not an evangelist either in the sense of Philip or by giftedness (Eph. 4:11). Otherwise, Paul would not have needed to exhort him to do such work.

Reflecting on our church, I can clearly see individuals who are more effective than others at bringing people to Christ. Roy is a prime example. It is as if he has one foot in the world and one foot in the church. He is what is referred to as a bridge-spanner. Roy effectively became a bridge spanning the gulf between our church and those outside. He develops strong relationships with families on his block by hosting swimming parties in his pool and Saturday evening movies on his lawn. He has been able to see the families on both sides of his house receive Christ and join our church. He is always bringing new people into our church.

Evaluation

Research shows that churches effectively proclaiming the gospel have three clearly defined ways of doing so. For some, it is a series of concerts where unchurched people gather to hear musical entertainment and are introduced to Christ through the testimonies of the musicians. In others, it is effective use of evangelistic Bible studies that offer a place for nonbelievers to hear the gospel in a nonthreatening manner. For some, it is the pastor explaining the gospel from the pulpit. For still others, it is programs of witness training.

However, for effective evangelism to take place in your

church you should have a minimum of three ways to proclaim the gospel. From the list of church ministries developed in the previous chapter write the ones that are strictly for proclaiming the good news (see fig. 5). Which of your ministries clearly presents the gospel? Trains your members to invite others?

So, what's your I.Q.? How do you score?

Note

[1]George Barna, *Marketing a Church* (Colorado Springs: Nav Press, 1988), 111.

Figure 5

3
Persuasion
Evangelism

Recently in the Southeast, hurricane Hugo unleashed tremendous destruction. Thousands of people were left homeless, businesses were lost, and several churches were inundated by the water and debris. Most of the inhabitants of these states were shocked that such a thing would ever happen to them.

The sad aftermath of Hugo left people cleaning and salvaging whatever they could. Insurance companies reported hundreds of requests for flood insurance policies, especially among those whose properties were not affected.

Many people agree that humanity is afflicted with the plague of procrastination. People usually refuse to do more preparation than is absolutely necessary. When disaster comes, the mad rush for protection begins. Unfortunately, this complacent attitude can also be seen in today's churches. People act the same way toward the second coming of Christ. They refuse to do any preparation beforehand. The ultimate problem for these people is that at His coming, there will be no second chances or insurance policies available.

I think it was with this burden that the apostle Paul wrote, "Therefore knowing the fear of the Lord, we persuade men, but we are made manifest to God; and I hope that we are made manifest also in your consciences" (2 Cor. 5:11).

The Art of Persuasion

Many churches today have heaven and earth all mixed up. They find themselves ministering only to Christians, enjoying one another's fellowship, but refusing to get involved with, or include, non-Christians in their activities. This is wrong. When we have the joy of being in glory together, we will have no more opportunities to persuade people. Those days will be gone, and we will have literally thousands of years to enjoy one another's company and fellowship. Living for today means that our priorities must include touching the lives of the unsaved.

Several years ago, a young couple called our church and asked if we would dedicate their newborn child. What is a pastor to do when given this opportunity? Talk about Jesus Christ, that's what! How can we talk about a young life being dedicated to Christ if the parents are not believers? The father accepted Christ. We, as a church, must get outside of ourselves. Jesus got outside of His close circle of friends and went to the unchurched to persuade them of who He was and what a difference He could make in their lives.

Once an unchurched person has moved through our funnel from an observer to a hearer, our next step is to move him or her to a believer. This takes persuasion. Persuasion involves training people to share their faith.

In Southern California a group of men and women at a rather small church wanted to go into their neighborhoods to invite people to church. None of the dozen people had ever shared their faith, but they were determined not to allow their feelings to inhibit their convictions.

"But what do we say?" The pastor told them simply to ask their neighbors what kind of church they would attend if they could find one in their community. Then tell them, "You realize, don't you, that going to church will not get you to heaven?" Friends, the neighborhood loved that. That is just what they wanted to hear. These committed twelve were going into their community speaking the world's language, "You don't have to go to church," and in two weekends each person had at least one friend to pick up for services on Sunday morning.

Training people to share their faith may be as simple as this story or it could be a full-blown course like Evangelism Explosion. Whatever it is, churches with effective persuasion train their people to share their faith.

Persuasion involves programs to win people to Christ. Many churches remind us of the farmer who is trying to gather his harvest while sitting in the toolshed. Every Sunday you see him in the toolshed, studying bigger and better methods of agriculture, sharpening his hoes, greasing his tractors, then going back in the house. In the evening, he will be back again to keep up-to-date on his skills. He does this week in and week out. Year in and year out. Yet he never gets into the fields to gather in the harvest. Churches that are effective in persuading people to come to Christ get out of the toolshed and put their tools to use.

Evaluation

As noted earlier, churches which are winning people to Christ have at least three program ways to persuade others to come to Christ. Look at your list of church ministries (from chapter 2) and write below the ones that focus on persuading people to accept Christ.

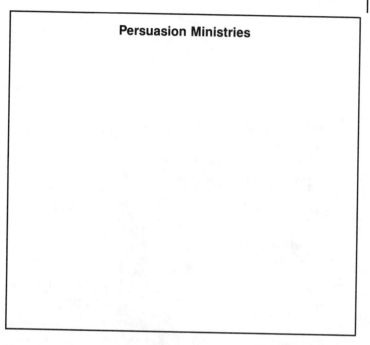

Persuasion Ministries

Transfer your persuasion ministries to figure 6 and identify the number of persuasion ministries still needed.

AN ONLOOKER

A HEARER

A BELIEVER

A LEARNER

A DISCIPLER

PRESENCE EVANGELISM

PROCLAMATION EVANGELISM

PERSUASION EVANGELISM

MINISTRIES IN PLACE

1. _____
2. _____
3. _____

MINISTRIES NEEDED

1. _____
2. _____
3. _____

EVANGELISM

Figure 6

4
Progression Evangelism

Once upon a time, there was a piece of iron which was very strong. Many attempts had been made to break it, but all had failed.

"I'll master it," said the ax. His blows fell heavily on the iron, but every blow made his edge more blunt until it ceased to strike.

"Leave it to *me*," said the saw. It worked backward and forward on the iron's surface until its jagged teeth were all worn and broken. Then it fell aside.

"Ah!" said the hammer, "I *knew* you wouldn't succeed. I'll show you the way." But at the first fierce blow, off flew its head and the iron remained as before.

"Shall *I* try?" asked the small, soft flame.

"Forget it," everyone else said. "What can *you* do?"

But the flame curled around the iron, embraced it, and never left the iron until it melted under the flame's irresistible influence.

As Jesus' disciples, our mission is not to *break* hearts but to melt them under the irresistible influence of God's infinite love.

We have seen already that the beginning avenue for evangelism is presence evangelism. We are called to carry one another's burdens and to meet one another's needs. The unchurched need to observe Christ in our lives. From there we move into the area of proclamation evangelism. Genuine disciples must tell others about

4 Christ. People must not only observe the gospel in our lives but hear it from our lips. Persuasion evangelism is the third mode of working with people where we remove the obstacles and share convictions. People should be persuaded to become believers, not just hearers and observers. Most churches think their evangelism strategy ends there. However, a broad view sees two additional steps in the overall plan for effective evangelism. The fourth strategy is progression evangelism, which we will focus on in this chapter.

In working cross-denominationally and across the country, I have noted several symptoms of our age.

> 1. *The call to "make disciples" is no longer a priority*—The church is facing a low ebb regarding a "Great Commission Consciousness." Many churches have created more of a country club than an army prepared and motivated to reach their world for Jesus Christ.
>
> 2. *More affirmation is given to events than to people*—When the potluck is over, we applaud the cooks. When the basketball team is victorious, we cheer the players. When was the last time that your church clapped and cheered for someone who has led someone else to Christ or is discipling a new convert?
>
> 3. *Follow-up is quickly becoming a lost art*— Where are all these people who have recently become a part of God's kingdom? The vast majority may be a part of the kingdom, but few become a part of the church. Win Arn's organization in California has provided some great insights into this factor.
>
> Research conducted by Church Growth Inc., Monrovia, California, on why people have come to

Christ and the Church, provides astonishing support on the oikos process at work today. Over 34,000 lay people have been asked the question: "What or who was responsible for your coming to Christ and your church?" One of the following eight responses was usually given: (1) some said a "special need" brought them to Christ and the church; (2) some responded they just "walked in"; (3) others listed the "pastor"; (4) some indicated "visitation"; (5) others mentioned the "Sunday School"; (6) a few listed "evangelistic crusade or television program"; (7) others recalled that the church "program" attracted them; (8) finally, some people responded "friend/relative" as being the reason they are now in Christ and the church.

What percentage of people came to their new relationship with Christ and their church through each category? Here are the results:

Special Need 1-2%
Walk-In 2-3%
Pastor 5-6%
Visitation 1-2%
Sunday School 4-5%
Evangelistic Crusade . . . . 1/2 of 1%
Church Program 2-3%
Friend/Relative . . . . 75-90%[1]

Notice the extremely low percentage of assimilated evangelistic crusade conversions compared to the friend/relative percentages. Apparently, the vast number of people who begin their pilgrimage with Christ and who have a person to encourage them in their growth end up as responsible members of the local church.

Churches which effectively win and hold new members have a plan for progression evangelism. Their plan normally involves three key ministries.

Ministry #1—A new believers' orientation (a way to introduce new believers to the faith).

Ministry #2—A new members' orientation (a way to challenge people to commit to their church).

Ministry #3—A focus on discipleship (a way to motivate people to grow in their walk with Christ).

Orientation of New Believers

Phil had come to a critical time in his life. His wife had left him and taken their two kids along. Alcohol was the predominant influence in his day-to-day experience, and he saw no hope. He came to the pastor of a growing church in hope that those things he had heard from his friends would prove to be true. Through the tears of anguish, he caught his first sight of the Lord of hope. Now, how could the church help him grow? The Sunday School courses were a little too advanced for Phil, he would get lost. The services were appealing and prayer meeting was a great time to get support, yet Phil would be intimidated since he didn't know how to pray. How would Phil ever learn to pray or study the Bible? How would the church tell Phil that the Bible is the owner's manual of his life? Orientation is vital to all new believers, and many seasoned Christians wish they could have had the same.

There are several ways of addressing the follow-up needs of new Christians. One possibility is training individuals to pray for new believers entrusted to their care—contacting them and staying with them until they are growing in Christ in the church.

Another successful method includes a small-group setting designed specifically for the young in faith. These "nurture groups" begin with the basics and progress into the normal curriculum of the small-group ministries which are addressed in a later chapter. These groups often stay together, mandating the need for a new nurture group to begin periodically to assimilate the latest converts. This same principle can be applied to a Sunday School environment as well. Either way, the most often covered issues include: Biblical Assurance, Testing and Temptations, Knowing the Will of God, Prayer, Forgiveness, Gifts of the Spirit, and Stewardship.

Commitment to a Local Church

Progression in faith naturally leads to responsible church membership. Yet haven't you been asked, "Can't I be a Christian without joining the church?" Yes, it is a possibility, but it would resemble the student who desires to learn but has no desire for school. It would be like the professional athlete who loves his sport, but has no desire to practice or train.

Throughout the New Testament, believers in Christ are viewed as "the called ones." This is a reference to a radical change in life that occurs when we fully come to grips with our relationship with Christ. This change should motivate us to identify ourselves with a local body which has similar dreams. A possible way of facilitating this progression is a new members' class. One church called theirs "The Three E's in Excitement" and covered such critical issues as evangelism, equipping, and encouragement. Other churches have sought to use this series of meetings to cover the direction of their church and its infrastructure. Many other churches with whom I have worked base their instruction around Ray Ortlund's conclusion, "My three life priorities are going to be—(1) God, (2) Believers, (3) My work in this world."[2]

Whatever the means, effective churches will have at least one way to help new believers become a part of their body.

Discipleship as a Focus

Robert Dale shares that "the first step in awakening a kingdom dream in a congregation is for the minister and key leaders to share a vision of the church."[3] He says that "methods vary for awakening a dream. But the dynamic remains constant: vision makes the difference in a congregation."[4] Any effective progression evangelism strategy includes discipleship as a part of the vision.

A disciple is merely a learner. He is open. He is teachable. He is one who understands the importance of quiet time and the Bible's influence in his life. He therefore has a consistent time of study which is systematic and self-applied.

Lyle Schaller writes that the major problem with this desire to become a disciple is the enormous amount of choices offered today. He illustrates:

> Once upon a time matters such as birth, death, the premature termination of a pregnancy, attendance at family reunions, marriage ending only with the death of your spouse, and the place where you will live were givens. Today each has become a matter of individual choice.[5]

With the myriad of choices comes a lack of commitment by people. Many today are uncommitted in giving, in church attendance, and in the desire to grow in their walk with Christ. Discipleship, as a focus, can motivate people to a state of accountability to continue their trek toward Christlikeness.

If you wander the aisles of a book store, you soon realize the diversity of discipleship programs. One of the most effective programs in wide use is the Navigators 2:7 Series. The Navigators 2:7 curriculum is having an incredible impact on churches. It is systematic and progresses from the basics all the way through the development of skills needed to lead others to Christ. Its weekly meetings are supported by about two hours of refreshing and challenging personal time.

There are a variety of one-on-one programs circulating as well. Each is designed to motivate Christians to sit under the guidance of another, more experienced disciple who will nurture them through the process of maturity. This approach is based upon Jesus' command, "Follow me," and Paul's instruction in 2 Timothy 2:2, "And the things which you have heard from me in the presence of many witnesses, these entrust to faithful men, who will be able to teach others also."

Progressing in our faith requires the mobilization of people meeting the needs of others. The process can be seen in a simple diagram:

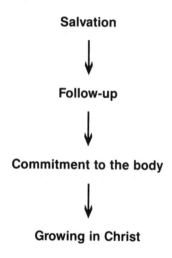

Salvation

↓

Follow-up

↓

Commitment to the body

↓

Growing in Christ

If the system falls short at any given point, the pilgrimage toward Christlikeness is short-circuited.

Evaluation

Like with presence, proclamation, and persuasion, a church needs to have three programs for reaching people via progression evangelism. From your list of church ministries (chapter 2), write in the following box the ones that are designed specifically to help people progress in their faith. Be careful. You may be tempted to list almost all of your church ministries. However, use only those which *specifically*

- follow up new believers,
- orient people to join church,
- disciple people in their faith.

```
┌─────────────────────────────────────────┐
│          Progression Ministries         │
│                                         │
│                                         │
│                                         │
│                                         │
│                                         │
│                                         │
│                                         │
│                                         │
│                                         │
└─────────────────────────────────────────┘
```

Now transfer these ministries to figure 7 and identify the number of ministries needed.

AN ONLOOKER

A HEARER

A BELIEVER

A LEARNER

A DISCIPLER

PRESENCE EVANGELISM

PROCLAMATION EVANGELISM

PERSUASION EVANGELISM

PROGRESSION EVANGELISM

MINISTRIES
IN PLACE
1. _____
2. _____
3. _____

MINISTRIES
NEEDED
1. _____
2. _____
3. _____

EVANGELISM

Figure 7

John F. MacArthur, Jr., once likened the impact that the Spirit of God can have on our lives to a Fizzie:

> A Fizzie is a small tablet used to make a soft drink; it's sort of a flavored Alka-Seltzer. Put it in a glass of water and its flavor releases throughout the water. This concentrated, compact power pill is no good as long as it sits on the bottom of the glass. It has to release its energy to fill the glass, and then it turns the water into something new. If it is a grape Fizzie, you get a glass of grape drink. The flavor of the tablet determines the flavor of the water.[6]

So why is it that so many Christians fizzle instead of radiating the divine power within? There is no progression evangelism, the essence of learning to allow God to release His power through our lives.

Notes

[1]Win Arn and Charles Arn, *The Master's Plan for Making Disciples* (Monrovia, Calif.: Church Growth Press, 1982), 43.

[2]Raymond C. Ortlund, *Lord, Make My Life a Miracle* (Ventura, Calif.: Regal Books, 1974), 4.

[3]Robert D. Dale, *To Dream Again* (Nashville: Broadman Press, 1981), 11.

[4]Ibid., 137.

[5]Lyle Schaller, *It's a Different World* (Nashville: Abingdon Press, 1987), 224.

[6]John F. MacArthur, Jr., *Keys to Spiritual Growth* (Old Tappan, N.J.: Revell, 1976), 73.

5
Production Evangelism

A father and his son stopped at a fast-food restaurant for something to eat one day. Dad wasn't all that hungry, so he ordered French fries for his young son and only a drink for himself. However, soon the aroma of the fries reached his nose, and he decided to sample a few.

He asked his son if he could have some. "No," said the child. Dad thought this was cute at first and asked once again. The child refused, pulling the bag of fries close to himself, protecting it with his arms. The father contemplated this experience: *Doesn't my son remember who gave him the French fries in the first place? Doesn't he realize that I have the physical power to take them away from him? Doesn't he see that I can give him more fries than he could ever imagine? My son is being selfish!*

Do you suppose that God has had similar thoughts about our churches? He has given us everything that we need. He has provided us with money, opportunities, talents, and relationships. He has given us spiritual gifts to do the work of the ministry. He even has given us time. But we fail to give some of our resources back to God when He asks. We have lost our perspective. Everything we have has been given to us by Him and He can take it away any time He wants.

A well-developed evangelism strategy moves people from observer to hearer to believer to learner.

Is that all there is? Do we stop here? No, we must go

one step further and examine the area of production evangelism—helping people become disciplers.

Helping people become disciplers means we must recognize that people have different roles in the discipling process. C. Peter Wagner observes, "In the average evangelical church, up to ten percent of the members have been given the gift of evangelism."[1] If this statement is true, then we cannot expect the entire congregation to be discipling the world as harvesters. There must be a healthy balance between planters, cultivators, and harvesters. The apostle Paul in his first letter to the Corinthian church explained,

> What then is Apollos? And what is Paul? Servants through whom you believed, even as the Lord gave opportunity to each one. I planted, Apollos watered, but God was causing the growth. So then neither the one who plants nor the one who waters is anything, but God who causes the growth. Now he who plants and he who waters are one; but each will receive his own reward according to his own labor. For we are God's fellow workers; you are God's field, God's building. (1 Cor. 3:5-9)

Let us examine the need for these three phases of production evangelism.

Planting

Evangelism must be seen as a process, taking one step at a time. E. Stanley Jones, the great evangelist and missionary to India, tells about a Chinese engineer:

> He sat down with me and abruptly said, "What are you going to do with me? I am a man without any religion. The old is dead and I haven't anything new to take its place. In America no church would take me, for I cannot believe in the divinity of

Christ." I could almost see him inwardly stiffen to meet my arguments to prove Christ divine. So I used none. Instead I asked, "What do you believe? How far along are you?" "Well," he said, "I can believe that Christ was the best of men." I said, "Then let us begin where you can. If He is the best of men, then He is your ideal. Are you prepared to act according to that idea? To cut out of your life everything that Christ would not approve?" "If I'm honest, then I must. And I will." I said, "Then whoever Christ turns out to be, man or more than man, wouldn't you be stronger and better if He were living with you, in you, all the time?" "Of course, I would be different." "Then you will let Him into your life." "I would not know how." "Then pray this prayer after me, sentence by sentence." He did. "This is different," he said, as he arose, "for they always told me I had to believe first. Now at least here is something for me to begin on." The next day he came again, his face radiant. "I didn't know a man could be as happy as I have been today. All my questions and doubts as to who Christ is have gone. And, moreover, I have been talking to my wife and she wants it too."[2]

Some people have the joy of being involved in more than one phase of the evangelism process, but most do not. Yet there is one aspect that all people can identify with and become involved with. This aspect is vital to any evangelistic strategy. It is inviting. Church members must have a strong desire to invite their friends, relatives, and acquaintances. Picture the church as a pyramid. Foundational to its production evangelism is the idea that we must be trained to invite people to church. Then our training must be applied as we invite others to church. I am convinced that 80 percent of all church membership should be trained in this facet of ministry (see fig. 8).

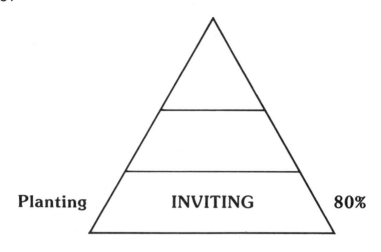

Figure 8

Can you remember the zeal that consumed your life when you first met Jesus Christ? It is almost a blind zeal that empowers us to tell others and share our newfound relationship with the risen Savior. This kind of blind, but cordial, zeal was seen in a young soldier who was on armed sentry duty for the first time. He had been given orders not to allow any cars onto the military base unless they bore a special identification seal. The first car to pull up without the special seal was carrying a general. When the general testily told his driver not to listen but to drive on through anyway, the sentry poked his head in the window and said politely, "I'm new at this, Sir. Who do I shoot first, you or the driver?"

When we first become Christians, we are on fire. What should we do? Why aren't we doing it? But as time passes, the seasoned veterans of the faith have had their zeal tempered, if not destroyed. We must rekindle the flame, and there are a myriad of ways of starting a spark.

"Friend Day" programs in churches have worked effectively. This is an established, nonthreatening approach to get people inviting others to church. In working with a church in Southern California that was on the verge of breaking the "two hundred barrier," I found that this approach was the springboard to a variety of other ministries. They were convinced that people would be "moved by the Spirit" if they would come to church. It was determined that goals had to be established first if there were to be any positive movement in the congregation. Bill Sullivan, a noted church-growth director writes,

> If you are going to break through the barrier, set a three-year goal that is well beyond the barrier and manageable within existing and available facilities. I suggest the goal be at least 300, and this small only if there is no way of handling a larger crowd in existing or available facilities. A goal of 300 is more than doubling and may appear very large if you're only running 115 to 120. I admit that there are times when doubling is not manageable, but in attempting to break the barrier, it is the only realistic goal.[3]

Three hundred became their realistic goal and this was almost exactly what they attained on their "Friend Day." Now the goal was visualized. Now the goal was grasped. "Yes, we can invite our friends."

Another church chose to take a different approach. They customized business cards that offered an invitation to come and worship, as well as giving times and directions. They challenged every member to pass out one card each week and provided each with fifty-two cards. Monitoring and affirmation are vital to this approach. The pastor interviewed new members from the pulpit to help the congregation see the effectiveness of the cards. This proved to be well received and motivated a large majority to become active in inviting other people to the church.

Cultivation

Invitations are an essential ingredient to production evangelism, but there also must be those who cross the line of commitment to be trained in the area of sowing. Planting involves inviting; sowing focuses in on friendship evangelism, and should include 50 percent of the church instructed in invitation (see fig. 9).

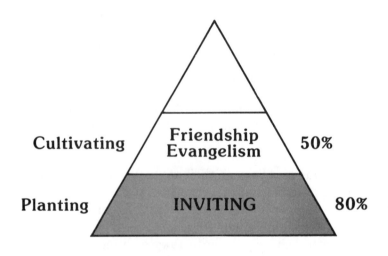

Figure 9

Ours is a skeptical age. Whom can we trust? Where do we turn for answers to life's toughest questions? The celebration of the 250th anniversary of the founding of Harvard University was climaxed by a great parade through the streets of Cambridge, Massachusetts. The parade was led by the president of the University, followed by dignitaries from the alumni, then the current senior, junior and sophomore classes. Finally, at the end of the parade, came members of the freshman class, carrying a large banner which read: HARVARD UNIVERSITY HAS WAITED 250 YEARS FOR US! Did it ever occur to you that our world has been waiting countless years for *You?* The church has been waiting nearly two thousand years for *You!* It is your time to parade your ideals and hopes and dreams and creativity and faith down the streets of your earthly pilgrimage. Joe Aldrich, president of Multnomah School of the Bible has stated it as clearly and pointedly as can be said:

> The world listens when Christians love. Consequently, the corporate image of the local church in its community is a critical factor in its evangelistic impact. In the final analysis, the church is both message and medium, exemplifying and proclaiming the kingdom of God. This truth has tremendous implications. At the very least, it is obvious that the church not exemplifying the kingdom is moribund and ineffective in the cause of world evangelization. Our world is full of professing Christians who claim to believe the truth, but are producing ugliness. They can't get along. They fight, gossip, and often act like they were weaned on dill pickles. Instead of being an "ambassador in" the world, they are an "embarrassment to" the world. They'll fight for the "truth," but have no grace. Truth has not failed. Instead, the edification process has somehow broken down.[4]

He adds:

> We are all "value vacuum cleaners." Our values are shaped by our associations. This principle

works both ways. If we treasure friendship with a person or group, we tend to become more and more alike as we mutually shape and reinforce each other's value systems. On the other hand, if we strongly dislike a person or group we tend to reject their values (whether right or wrong). Thus our values are socially anchored. The choices we make are influenced by these socially anchored values.[5]

The Scriptures validate these principles. The woman at the well was first accepted, then introduced. Paul dares the early believers to "imitate me." How is it that all men will know that we are His disciples? What is the goal of our instruction? Is it not love? The healthy, virile church is one that places a premium on friendships as an evangelistic tool and offers a curriculum that provides training in this area.

Campus Crusade for Christ has been one of the prime movers in this arena. Their "Jesus" film and the accompanying training curriculum have been successful in creating a safe environment for discussion and debate. Grace Community Church in Panorama City, California, offers a full-blown curriculum entitled "Friendship Evangelism" written by Jim George. Jim has provided ample instruction regarding fear, persuasion, and the challenge of witnessing with your life-style.

Harvesting

Effective people tend to rise to the top. This will be true in your production evangelism efforts. We have already determined that 80 percent of your church should be inviting people to church functions or services. We have also determined that 50 percent of these will rise to a higher level of leadership as they become trained in friendship evangelism. Yet remember there is a higher level of leadership, a level committed to the task of harvesting the fields. Here we find, as previously stated, approximately 10 percent of the church body who are the soul winners and have the gift of evangelism (see fig. 10).

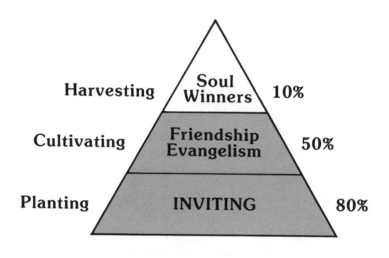

Figure 10

Evaluation

Churches which effectively train evangelistic disciplers do so by three program methods. From your list of church ministries (chapter 2) write on the following page the ones which specifically train people to

- Plant
- Cultivate
- Harvest

Production Ministries

From the list above, transfer the production ministries to figure 11 and identify the number of Production Evangelism Ministries still needed.

Not every church member will be a soul winner. Neither will all the people in your church get involved in friendship evangelism. The following story shares that each of us must do what we can, however.

A young Christian in Seattle, Washington, saw a man handing out tracts in a busy downtown area. The distributor had a satchel full of tracts which he gave out rapidly without stopping to engage in conversation. *Why doesn't he talk with someone?* thought the observing Christian. *His method is so cold and impersonal.*

Finally, unable to stand it any longer, the young Christian approached the distributor from behind. Turn-

Figure 11

ing him around by his collar and looking into his face, he asked, "Why don't you speak to someone about the Savior?"

The fellow blurted out, "Ugh—ugh—ugh!" He couldn't speak. He was a mute. But he was doing what he could.

Notes

[1]C. Peter Wagner, *How to Grow a Church* (Ventura, Calif.: Regal, 1976), 86.

[2]E. Stanley Jones, *Victorious Living* (Nashville: Abingdon Press, 1977).

[3]Bill M. Sullivan, *Breaking the 200 Barrier* (Kansas City: Beacon Hill Press, 1988), 36.

[4]Joseph C. Aldrich, *Life-Style Evangelism* (Portland: Multnomah Press, 1981), 101.

[5]Ibid., 103.

Evaluation
Develop Your
Evangelism
Strategy

Pastor Bob began his ministry with a commitment to immediate outreach. He began with a Sunday afternoon class to train willing church members to share their faith aggressively. Drawing from the best of Evangelism Explosion, Campus Crusade, and Navigator materials, he put together a sixteen-week curriculum that rivaled the best. He developed his materials further by visiting other churches to find out what was working elsewhere. After fine-tuning his program, members were recruited and the course began.

Each class was a mix of training, role playing, and a real call on past visitors to the church. The main objective was to share the gospel of Jesus Christ. Pastor Bob often said, "If you are able to share the gospel, you are a success. If you leave without sharing the gospel, you have failed."

Careful records were kept. After sixteen weeks, the results were tallied.

> 52 visits attempted
> 48 visits made
> 32 complete gospel presentations
> 1 person prayed for salvation
> 0 people brought into the church

What had gone wrong? Church members were trained. The gospel was shared. But few results could be seen. While all of the members were excited, the clear truth could not be ignored. Their best training, their best motives, and their best efforts had not helped this church become effective at winning people to Christ.

Review Your Evangelism Strategy

Look carefully at your church's overall evangelism strategy. The following questionnaire will help you think through your strategy objectively. Answer each question honestly. This is not the time to fudge on your answers. You need to be frank and perhaps even ruthless when evaluating your church.

Circle the correct answer to each question:

Question	*Answer*
1. Is our church known for at least one ministry in our community?	YES NO
2. Are our church members regularly inviting their family, friends, and associates to our church?	YES NO
3. Does our church have a class in which members develop their personal testimony?	YES NO
4. Does our church have a class in which new believers are taught the basics of the Christian faith?	YES NO
5. Does our church have a process by which members list the names of unchurched friends and begin praying for their salvation?	YES NO

6. Does our church have at least one ministry which directly touches a felt need of unchurched people in our community?   YES   NO

7. Does our church have a planned way to help new visitors find their way around our church?   YES   NO

8. Does our church have a means by which members are taught to verbalize their faith?   YES   NO

9. Does our church have a course whereby new people are orientated to our church?   YES   NO

10. Does our church have a way to train members to develop friendships with the unchurched?   YES   NO

11. Does our church have at least four events each year targeted specifically to unchurched people?   YES   NO

12. Does our church have a way of welcoming visitors to our church which does not embarrass them?   YES   NO

13. Does our church have at least one ministry that is effectively winning new people to Christ?   YES   NO

14. Does our church have at least one program that is aimed at helping new people grow in their faith?   YES   NO

15. Does our church have at least one ministry that trains members to be assertive in sharing their faith?   YES   NO

Tally your answers below by checking the box beside each question answered YES above. Then add up the checked boxes across and place the number of checked boxes on the line at the right of each series.

Questions			Total	Strategy
1 ☐	6 ☐	11 ☐	___	Presence
2 ☐	7 ☐	12 ☐	___	Proclamation
3 ☐	8 ☐	13 ☐	___	Persuasion
4 ☐	9 ☐	14 ☐	___	Progression
5 ☐	10 ☐	15 ☐	___	Production

Grand Total ___

1- 5 points = Poor: Overall unbalanced strategy
6-10 points = Good: Strong in some areas, weak in others
11-15 points = Excellent: Overall balanced strategy

Develop Your Evangelism Strategy

You completed the funnel model as you read each chapter. Take a moment now to transfer your findings from figures 4, 5, 6, 7, and 11 to figure 12. Take a close look to see where your overall evangelism strategy is strong and where it is weak.

Your evangelism strategy is strong if each of the five areas has three ministries listed. Your strategy is good if there are two listed for each area and poor if each area has one or even no ministry listed. Possibly, your evangelism strategy is strong in one or two areas and weak in the others. For example, you might have three ministries under persuasion and progression but almost none under the remaining three.

Take a moment to review your completed model. In the following box, briefly describe your church's overall

---

Overall Evangelism Strategy

---

evangelism strategy. Where are your strengths? Where are your weaknesses?

In previous chapters, to the right of the evangelism funnel, you listed some ideas for ministries that are needed and could be developed. In the box below, briefly summarize what ministries you need to have a balanced evangelism strategy.

Needed Ministries

Most churches are only able to develop one new ministry each year. On occasion a church may be able to start two or three, depending on the available leadership and other resources. However, normally a church would be foolish to begin more than one new ministry from scratch in a given year. A church may be able to retool an existing ministry with less effort than beginning a new one. Thus, in developing the following plan, perhaps you should plan on starting no more than one new ministry per year plus retooling one other.

In the following chart prioritize the new ministries your church needs. Note who could begin to develop the ministry and the date that you would like for it to begin.

Summary

From your plans above finish the model in figure 12 by adding your plans to the far right column. You should now have a complete view of your evangelism strategy.

The funnel shows you the process by which new people will come to Christ and experience growth through your church's ministries. The first column lists the ministries you currently have in place for each critical area. The second column shows the ministries that are needed to strengthen your evangelism. The third column shows your plans to begin new ministries over the next five years.

	MINISTRY	AREA	LEADER	DATES
1				
2				
3				
4				
5				

FINDING THEM – EVALUATING YOUR CHURCH

Figure 12

Part 2
*Keeping
Them:
Assimilation*

6
Assimilation Through Friendship

Longfellow said, "Ah, how good it feels, the hand of an old friend." Emerson said, "A friend may well be reckoned the masterpiece of Nature." Franklin said it this way, "There are three faithful friends—an old wife, an old dog, and ready money." Cicero said, "Friendship adds a brighter radiance to prosperity and lightens the burden of adversity by dividing and sharing it." Solomon said in Proverbs 18:24, "A man of many friends comes to ruin, But there is a friend who sticks closer than a brother."

Visitors to the Florida home of Thomas A. Edison will find a unique stone walkway in his garden. He called it his "friendship walk." Each stone was dedicated by a friend. The stones reminded him that friends were the means of his success.

Assimilation begins right at the heart of our need for relationships. Many churches are inclusive in outreach, yet exclusive in fellowship. People can be reached, baptized, and brought into membership and not be incorporated into the friendship structure of a church.

Lyle E. Schaller writes in *Assimilating New Members:*

> The background theory is that every congregation can be described in terms of two concentric circles. The larger outer circle is the membership circle.

> Every member is within that outer circle. The smaller inner circle includes the members who feel a sense of belonging and who feel fully accepted into the fellowship of that called-out community. Most of the leaders come from persons within this fellowship circle. By contrast, many of the workers who do not have policy-making authority may be drawn from among the members who are outside the fellowship circle. In some congregations workers may even be recruited from among the people who are outside the membership circle, some of whom identify with this congregation as constituents and some of whom are members of other congregations. One of the means of distinguishing between those within the fellowship circle and those outside it is the terminology; the former usually are comfortable with the pronouns we, us, and ours when referring to that congregation, while the latter tend to use they, them, and theirs more frequently.[1]

The essence of his research shows that there are two distinct and separate levels of inclusion. One is the superficial level to which most Christians find themselves belonging. This is a level where they feel comfortable in the worship service, but where Sunday School or small-group involvement is avoided, and service and support are not on the agenda.

The second level is much more relational, and far more significant in the life of an assimilated member. It is the level where there is a sense of belonging and even a sense of accountability. It is the level where involvement in small-group ministries and service is an active part of the Christian life.

Development of this second level must be a continual focus of the leadership of a church. Schaller notes:

There is considerable evidence which suggests that at least one-third, and perhaps as many as one-half, of all protestant church members do not feel a sense of belonging to the congregation of which they are members. They have been received into membership, but have never felt they have been accepted into the fellowship circle.

Evangelism and receiving new members into a congregation are two separate actions.[2]

Just as evangelism can be seen as a massive funnel through which all people travel on their journey to responsible, productive, church members, the funnel illustration is again appropriate in your understanding of the assimilated members of your church (see fig. 13).

Notice that the beginning of this process, the heart of the issue, is friendship. This basic ingredient tends to spill over onto the other vital relationships in a person's life. Alan Loy McGinnis writes:

People with no friends usually have a diminished capacity for sustaining any kind of love. They tend to go through a succession of marriages, be estranged from various family members, and have trouble getting along at work. On the other hand, those who learn how to love their friends tend to make long and fulfilling marriages, get along well with the people at work, and enjoy their children.[3]

The Pillars of Friendship

Think of friendship as having six foundational pillars. The structure will stand with only five. It could even remain intact with four. But a real friend, the kind of

FRIENDSHIPS

TASKS / ROLES

SMALL GROUP

IDENTIFICATION

SPIRITUAL GROWTH

ASSIMILATION

Figure 13

friend that people need in our churches, has six characteristics:

> **F**un to be with
> **R**elational
> **I**nspiring
> **E**ncouraging
> **N**urturing
> **D**evoted

As we examine each of these pillars, think about your church environment and the friends that you have there. Are these characteristic of your friends? Are you providing the necessary programming and planning that enable people in your church to make these kinds of friends?

The first pillar simply tells us that your friend is fun to be with. Friendship is fun. People need to be in each other's company to laugh and play together. They need to play games and go for walks. The church must provide opportunities where people with common interests can come together and have fun. Be creative—sports teams, game nights, picnics at the lake, caroling parties, potlucks, film nights, hiking groups, camp outs, tennis tournaments—the list can be endless.

Despite the fun that must accompany genuine friendship, a second pillar of a deepening relationship must be developed. Scripture calls this depth of relationship love, a selfless expression of meeting the other's needs with no desires or expectations. This is a love that motivates us to cut through the layers of vulnerability and fear, and demonstrate real concern from the heart. This requires a willingness to be available to each other. When times are the toughest, each of us needs an "advocate," a person to come alongside and hold us up. We all need that circle of friends who know the real us and love us anyway. They accept us and they trust us.

Friendship demands sharing and trusting with the supreme motivation of love. Where can this relational side of friendship be developed? In many areas. Sunday School is a wonderful place for the relational mode of friend-making. Another vital area to this process is that of small groups, which will be discussed in greater detail in a later chapter.

The third pillar to cultivating a friendship is an inspiring relationship. No two people are alike. Proverbs 27:17 tells us, "Iron sharpens iron, So one man sharpens another." We all need sharpening and friends invigorate us to desire change in our lives.

In many of the churches where I have spoken and consulted, the one place where I have seen the invigorating nature of friendships more than any other is in discipleship groups. The Navigators 2:7 is an ideal example. People come together, accountable for memorization and Bible study, and motivate one another to keep with the program. Why do you think Alcoholics Anonymous is so successful? How has Weight Watchers had such an impact on the weight-loss scene? It is because of invigoration, what Webster says provides "vigor, vitality, or strength to."

The fourth pillar is encouragement. Have you ever been in a great mood only to have "Mr. Depressed" walk into your life? How did you feel when he left? The survival rate for a friendship where one person continually drags the other down is very poor. In the midst of our fun and our relationships and even our invigoration, there must be the desire to encourage each other. Encouragement allows the sun to peek through the clouds. Encouragement doesn't need to be flashy. In our church we have several ladies who provide encouragement by sending little notes. Do you know how good I feel when a note of thanks arrives on my desk? We also have a tradition for all new parents in the church. The Sunday after a child is born, we ask Dad to come forward and tell us about the new arrival and receive from the pastor a rose bud to give to Mom. Simple? Yes! Encouraging, knowing that the church is thinking of you when you are so tired? Very much so!

The fifth pillar is nurture. "Greater love has no one than this, that one lay down his life for his friends" (John 15:13). Real friendship needs nurture, the desire to give, give, and still give. The giving, nurturing side of friendship has two sides, sacrifice and spirituality. If we examine our friendships, it is not long before we can see the sacrifices we make. We may give up a Friday evening to watch the kids of our friends so they can have a night out. We could cancel our vacation if a pressing need arose. We should be ready to rearrange our schedules for the benefit of our friends.

The spiritual side of nurturing is much more involved. Rick was a young man in our church with a lot of potential. He had many friends and was seeking the opportunity to go into ministry. But his follow through was inconsistent. All of his life, he had been told to do whatever he wanted and not to feel bad when his commitments faltered. He found himself drifting away from God because he spent most of his time having fun with his newly developed circle of friends. What Rick really needed was a Christian friend who would love him enough to nurture him through these tough times and steer him back to spiritual things.

Flavell Yeakley has determined statistically that each of us needs at least seven friends if we are to stay in a church.[4] What may be even more alarming is that we may need an equal number of Christian friends to nurture us in our faith.

The last pillar is devotion. Proverbs 19:4-7 expresses what happens to friendships based on the wrong devotion.

Wealth adds many friends, But a poor man is separated from his friend. A false witness will not go unpunished, And he who tells lies will not escape. Many will entreat the favor of a generous man, And every man is a friend to him who gives gifts. All the brothers of a poor man hate him; How much more do his friends go far from him! He pursues them with words, but they are gone.

A Biblical Example

Nothing takes the place of true friendship. Especially rare are the people who are friends for life and who stand by you to the very end. Jesus had a few friends like that. One of them was the beloved apostle John, from that inner circle of disciples, who stood with Him even at His death on the cross. That friendship enabled our Lord to turn His mother, Mary, over to John's care. Also, Jesus revealed Himself to John during the last hours of John's life, when he was exiled on the island of Patmos. They were friends to the very end.

David had one true friend—Jonathan, Saul's son. Nothing could break their relationship. Jonathan and David promised friendship to one another, the kind of devotion that continues despite the troubles of life.

Jonathan appears for the first time in Scripture as a soldier who had already commanded a thousand troops at Gibeah (1 Sam. 13:2) and had led a charge against the Philistines (13:8 to 14:15). He had to be old enough to be a military veteran.

Now David, the son of Jesse, was still at home while several of his brothers were already in the army. He was a shepherd and even after he volunteered to fight Goliath, he was reminded, ". . . for you are but a youth" (17:33).

Whatever their ages, they met and soon after David's encounter with Goliath, this friendship blossomed into a real love for one another. "Now it came about when he had finished speaking to Saul, that the soul of Jonathan was knit to the soul of David, and Jonathan loved him as himself" (18:1). Interestingly, Jonathan was the heir apparent to the throne. However, because of Saul's disobedience and sin, the right of family succession was forfeited. Instead, David was chosen by God to be king. Saul was jealous. He realized that a friendship had developed between Jonathan and David. There was only one thing to do: Kill David and the throne would once again be Jonathan's.

But Jonathan and David had made a covenant, a binding, loyal commitment to each other. Jonathan knew that he would never be king and was willing to encourage his devoted friend and deliver him from his father's hand.

True friendship is a blessing. We would be fortunate to have a friend like Jonathan. But we, as a church, must provide ample opportunities for these types of bonds to develop.

Evaluation

A church which is effective in incorporating new people into its social structure will be able to identify a minimum of three distinct ways in which it does so. Take a few moments and list below all of the ways that your church provides to help people make friends in your church.

Transfer to figure 14 the names of programs and/or ministries that your church is now using to help new people make friends. Then list ministries that you need to start so that you will have a better incorporation strategy.

Ministries of Developing Friends

While practicing law, George G. Vest, a former U.S. senator from Missouri, defended a farmer whose dog was involved in a minor damage suit. Here is part of his speech:

> The one absolutely unselfish friend that man can have in this selfish world, the one that never proves ungrateful or treacherous, is his dog . . . . When all other friends desert, he remains. When riches take wings and reputation falls to pieces, he is as constant in his love as the sun in its journey through the heavens.
>
> If fortune drives the master forth an outcast in the world, friendless and homeless, the faithful dog asks no higher privilege than that of accompanying him to guard against danger, to fight against his enemies.
>
> And, when the last scene of all comes, and death

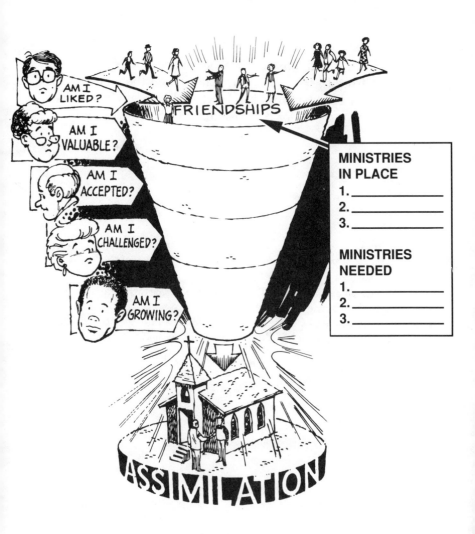

Figure 14

takes the master in his embrace, and his body is laid away in the cold ground, at grave side will be found the noble dog, his head between his paws, his sad eyes alert and watchful, still faithful and true even in death.

With this impassioned plea, Vest won a favorable verdict from the jury. I believe that when the same can be said for us, when that kind of devotion exists in our lives, we will experience real friendship.

Notes

[1]Lyle E. Schaller, *Assimilating New Members* (Nashville: Abingdon Press, 1978).

[2]Ibid., 16.

[3]Alan Loy McGinnis, *The Friendship Factor* (Minneapolis: Augsburg Publishing House), 9.

[4]Win Arn and Charles Arn, *The Master's Plan for Making Disciples* (Monrovia, Calif.: Church Growth Press, 1982), 156.

7
Assimilation Through Tasks/Roles

A man was driving on a lonely road one summer day. He saw a car with a flat tire pulled over on the shoulder of the road. Beside the car stood a woman looking down in dismay at the flat tire. The man decided to pull over and play the good Samaritan. He grew hot and sweaty and dirty in the hot sun as he changed the tire. The woman was watching him and just as he finished she said, "Be sure and let the jack down easily now because my husband is sleeping in the backseat of the car!" Cute story? Yes, but not too funny when you apply it to the church. Many of the people who leave the church disenchanted leave because no one had challenged them to wake up, climb out of the backseat, and help change the tire.

In recent years, an emphasis on church growth has awakened a new desire to discover and understand spiritual gifts. Scripture is clear that Christians are the Body of Christ on earth. We are a living organism with Christ as the head. Each part of the body must function to remain healthy. Equally important is the understanding that when a Christian exercises his or her spiritual gift in a role or task within the church, there is a much greater potential for assimilation.

C. Peter Wagner provides a workable definition for a spiritual gift. "A spiritual gift is a special attribute given by the Holy Spirit to every member of the Body of

Christ according to God's grace for use within the context of the Body."[1] Gifts are for the common good, not for individual attention or to enhance one's ego. Paul shared, "But to each one is given the manifestation of the Spirit for the common good" (1 Cor. 12:7). When these spiritual abilities are discovered and used for the benefit of others, three distinct contributions are added to the local church.

First, the members are edified. Why did the Spirit of God provide these spiritual gifts in the first place? Ephesians delivers ample insight: "And He gave some as apostles, and some as prophets, and some as evangelists, and some as pastors and teachers, for the equipping of the saints for the work of service to the building up of the body of Christ" (4:11-12). Spiritual gifts are the skills and abilities necessary to do the Master's work on earth, resulting in the maturation of the church.

The practical outworking of this principle is seen most clearly in the Book of Acts. The initial manifestation of the Spirit on the day of Pentecost, followed by Peter's Spirit-filled preaching, brought three thousand new members into the church (2:41). The regular wonders and signs done through the apostles (v. 43) meant that day by day the Lord added to the church those who were being saved (v. 47). The healing of the lame man at the Beautiful Gate of the Temple and the preaching of Peter that followed brought membership to about five thousand (4:4). Peter then exercised his gift of knowledge, which in turn enabled him to expose the hidden sins of Ananias and Sapphira. The result: More believers were added to the Lord, "multitudes of men and women" (5:14). Was it not the martyrdom of Stephen that led to evangelism in Samaria, and a little later, to the conversion of Saul? And so the connection continued. As members of the early church were willing to exercise all the gifts that were available to them, the church was edified and grew in number and strength.

Second, the members have their needs met. The importance of understanding the place of spiritual gifts within the life and the witness of the church as a whole cannot be overstressed. This emphasizes value for others, rather than for the individual Christian exercising. Leslie Flynn tells us "we are saved to serve."[2] Haven't you ever tried to figure out why God hasn't taken you home yet? He has things for you to do here, that's why. Jesus wrote, "It is not so among you, but whoever wishes to become great among you shall be your servant" (Matt. 20:26). What did He mean? Our Lord shared that greatness is not the result of being served, but through serving, by ministering to others.

Third, members are satisfied. The use and expression of spiritual gifts is but the beginning of this aspect of retention and assimulation. All humans need to contribute. Those who contribute manifest a much greater desire to stay while those who choose not to volunteer drop out more frequently. People need to feel fulfilled in their tasks. Ample evidence has been accumulated to support this concept. James G. Hougland and James Wood conclude that people who definitely feel that they are having an impact on their social structure will not only sense more satisfaction but also desire to continue their efforts.[3]

George Barna put it this way, "Unless you become involved in the activities of your church, you will never truly feel satisfied with that church."[4]

In 1979, Dean Hoge and David Roozen took on the monumental task of examining 225 inactive Presbyterians and 225 active Presbyterians. Their conclusions showed that both the inactives and actives were well versed in doctrine, but that despite a greater degree of disagreement on the part of the inactives, this had little to do with their drop-out rates.[5] Carl Dudley followed this study by determining that, "Generally, membership drop-outs were far more apt to leave in boredom than in disagreement."[6]

Win Arn, who is considered to be the foremost communicator in the field of church growth, has established workable ratios that offer us a plumb line to measure effective assimilation by way of tasks and roles. He first offers a simple definition: "A role/task refers to a specific position, function, or responsibility in the church (choir, committee member, teacher, officer, etc.)."[7] Arn observes that the typical church that is declining has approximately twenty-seven tasks/roles per every hundred adults in the church. In a declining church often those who are participants perform more than one task or role. This further limits the actual total number of participants. Arn's studies have also demonstrated that churches which have plateaued have developed forty-three opportunities to become involved per every hundred adults. The growing and healthy body offers sixty tasks or roles per every hundred adults, with a low level of overlap and overuse. Now these tasks are not "busy work, but Kingdom work. These new roles/tasks should focus on meeting needs, changing lives, and touching people with Christ's love and care."[8]

One of the great joys that I have seen in the growing church is that many of the necessary sixty roles/tasks per each hundred adults are created as church members see needs and respond by developing a ministry to meet those needs. We must come to grips with the same approach that Frank Tillapaugh has used at Bear Valley Baptist Church for years: "The Body can be trusted to produce what it needs."[9] The church finds its greatest expression in serving. Jesus said, "Just as the Son of Man did not come to be served, but to serve, and to give His life a ransom for many" (Matt. 20:28). Leadership should never forget this principle. Volunteers in our churches are waiting for opportunities.

In a recent edition of our *Church Growth Network* newsletter several implications were addressed looking to lead the church into the 1990s.

1. *People give/volunteer where there is a need*—Stress the importance of reaching our communities for Jesus Christ through meeting needs. Visualize the need you are asking people to support. Tell people how their involvement will change lives.

2. *People give/volunteer when asked to make a written commitment*—Ask people to anonymously fill out a yearly commitment card that is between God and themselves. Ask them to put it in a place of prominence in their lives as a constant reminder of their promise.

3. *People give/volunteer to values and goals rather than guilt and judging*—Solicit support and service based on your goals. People will participate longer and sense a greater degree of fulfillment when they realize that there is a reason for the hard work.

4. *People give/volunteer to causes that attract their interest*—Offer a variety of opportunities where people may serve. Present several ways for people to give. Allow people to give to different ministries. Focus on recruiting people to serve before asking for their financial gifts.

5. *People give/volunteer best through personal contact*—Challenge people to give and serve through personal invitation. Schedule meetings in homes, over lunch, or in small groups for presenting your church's needs. Host small dessert meetings for discussion of needs and recruitment for service.[10]

Evaluation

As a basic rule of thumb, growing churches will have a minimum of 60 percent of their members involved in an identifiable ministry role. Smaller churches may actually have more than 60 percent involvement while very large churches may find they fit the typical 80/20 rule—20 percent doing the work for the remaining 80 percent.

Churches with effective assimilation of new people typically have a number of ministries in place:

Ministry #1—A way to help new people identify their gifts and become involved in service.

Ministry #2—A number of entry level places of service.

Ministry #3—A flexible spirit that allows (even encourages) the beginning of new ministries.

In the following box, briefly describe your church's effectiveness in assimilating new people into service roles. Ask yourself the following questions:

1. Does my church have entry level places of service where new people are allowed to serve?

2. Does my church have an effective way to help people identify their gifts, talents, and abilities?

3. During the past three years, have at least 60 percent of our new members found a place to serve?

4. Has my church started at least one new ministry per year for the past three years?

Assimilation Effectiveness

Transfer to figure 15 the programs that your church presently has in place to assimilate new members/attenders into ministry roles/tasks. Then list some new ministries that you would like to start in the next few years.

I see many churches with the "flat-tire syndrome" discussed at the beginning of this chapter. We must awaken our sleeping members and get them out of the backseat so they can open the trunk, get the spare, and change the flat tire.

Notes

[1]C. Peter Wagner, *Your Spiritual Gifts Can Help Your Church Grow* (Ventura, Calif.: Regal Books, 1979), 42.

[2]Leslie B. Flynn, *19 Gifts of the Spirit* (Wheaton: Victor Books, 1983), 11.

[3]James G. Hougland and James Wood, "Control in Organizations and the Commitment of Members," *Social Forces,* 59 (September 1980): 93.

[4]George Barna, *How to Find Your Church* (Minneapolis: Worldwide Publications, 1989), 93.

[5]Dean R. Hoge and David A. Roozen, "Research on Factors Influencing Church Commitment," *Understanding Church Growth and Decline 1950-1978* (New York: The Pilgrim Press, 1979), 65.

[6]Carl S. Dudley, *Where Have All Our People Gone?: New Choices for Old Churches* (New York: The Pilgrim Press, 1979), 78.

[7]Win Arn, *The Church Growth Ratio Book* (Pasadena: Church Growth Inc., 1987), 10.

[8]Ibid., 68.

[9]Frank R. Tillapaugh, *Unleashing the Church* (Ventura, Calif.: Regal Books, 1982), 78.

[10]Glen S. Martin, "Giving and Volunteering in the 1990's," *The McIntosh Church Growth Network,* December 1989, 2.

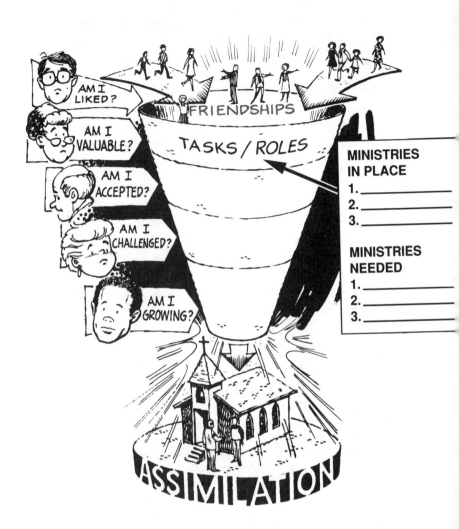

Figure 15

8
Assimilation Through Small Groups

The early church often met from house to house. What better way could there have been to cultivate the gladness and singleness of heart, the praising of God, and the favor of all the people that saw the Lord adding to the church daily those who should be saved (Acts 2:46-47)? Obviously, there were no modern Sunday Schools, no men's ministries or missionary societies, no boys' or girls' clubs, and no schedule of regular services as we know them today. There were no church buildings. In fact, the church at Jerusalem could not even meet in one home. Whose living room would have held more than five thousand people? Large gatherings of believers were reserved for the streets and the temple.

But the church of the first century is gone! I know you hate to hear that, but it's true; it cannot be revived. However, there are some distinctions of the early church which God intends for today's church. Small groups can add four key essential ingredients to the assimilation mix.

Sharing

> A good character is the best tombstone. Those who loved you, and were helped by you, will remember you when forget-me-nots are withered. Carve your name on hearts, and not on marble.—*Charles H. Spurgeon*[1]

Have you ever sat in a group setting and discussed only the superficial issues of life? "How was your day?" "Fine, and yours?" "Oh, . . . fine." That kind of strangling chitchat doesn't stimulate a desire to return to that setting again. We are relational beings. We were created in God's image with a yearning to commune with God, and with other relational beings. We long to know and to be known on levels transcending the superficial plane. A small group must provide more for a person than eight to twelve people sitting around eating cookies and drinking red punch.

Karen and Gary were a young couple in search of a place to share. Their lives had been riddled with confusion, pain, and desperation. Now they were searching for a place that they could not only learn but be accepted.

Gary had been overseas in the military and now was stationed in the States. Through many transfers, Karen had reached a point where she was afraid to have intimate friends. They came to my church, like many couples, making a plea to be known and accepted. When they completed the membership class, they were immediately plugged into a small group of couples their age.

After three to six months, they began to open up. Karen's fear of rejection was eliminated by the group's acceptance of her as she shared the disappointments of their continually shifting life-style. Karen and Gary soon learned that sharing is the heartbeat of a group. It helps people become vulnerable to one another and begins a process of "bearing one another's burdens."

Study

To read the Bible is to take a trip to a fair land where the spirit is strengthened and faith renewed.—*Dwight D. Eisenhower*[2]

Isn't that the truth! It is when the Bible becomes alive to a person that transformation can take place.

To study biblically is to renew your mind. "And do not be conformed to this world, but be transformed by the renewing of your mind, that you may prove what the will of God is, that which is good and acceptable and perfect" (Rom. 12:2). The body of believers is the vehicle through which this new life is expressed. We do not cultivate the body like the ancient Greeks who worshiped its beauty and strength. We do not crucify the body like the early ascetics who considered it evil and starved or mutilated it. We simply consecrate the body by "renewing [our] mind" to the illumination provided by the Holy Spirit. When this study occurs, what happens? Three things.

First, the student is changed morally. "And do not be conformed to this world." Every day there is pressure on all of us, not only in such relatively minor matters as dress and diet, but in such far more serious areas of life as morals, ethical standards, and religious beliefs. Small groups are a place where we can hear the Word of Christ (Rom. 10:17). They are a place where we can be molded from within rather than from without. There the believer has the inward power to overcome the pressures of the world.

Second, the student is changed mentally. "But be transformed by the renewing of your mind." This is a call for a transfigured life. The Greek word translated "transformed" in this passage occurs in only three other places in the New Testament. It is used to describe the transfiguration of the Lord Jesus (Matt. 17:2; Mark 9:2), and it is used to describe the glorious change wrought in believers when they steadfastly contemplate the Lord Jesus (2 Cor. 3:18). The Greek word is *metamorphoo* from which our word *metamorphosis* is derived. The dictionary defines metamorphosis as "a transformation, as by supernatural means; a marked alteration in appearance, condition, character, or function." The caterpillar, which undergoes metamorphosis, emerges as a glorious butterfly. The same creature which enters a filmy tomb eventually emerges, but the change is so remarkable that it cannot be recognized as the same. It is the kind of change that the Holy Spirit wishes to work in the life of the believer.

Last, the student is changed motivationally. "That you may prove what the will of God is, that which is good and acceptable and perfect." Only through study can we see God's direction for our lives and become motivated to walk in the steps that He has laid before us. Each person in a small group learns to study with anticipation, so that in the group there will be participation and outside the group there will be application.

Support

Nothing happens to you that hasn't happened to someone else.—*William Feather*[3]

We have implied throughout these opening chapters that real religion is always triangular—it cannot forget three centers of gravity—God, ourselves, and other people. Support is living in touch with people and closing the triangle.

The people who have the greatest impact upon others always seem to have two initial characteristics. First, they consistently portray an immense joy in living. That will always draw others who want to be around people who are happy to be alive. Enthusiasm is contagious. Second, they drop anything to help another person. Their bags lie unpacked, letters lie unanswered, the house is not cleaned, for as long a time as other people need. They are individual-conscious, not thing-conscious.

Small groups can contribute to overcoming this preoccupation with things and create within us the desire to "build up one another." First, we must face up to the fact that most other means of congregational support seldom experience success. Support is more than being a "good influence." We have all heard Emerson's remark that, "What you are stands over you the while, and thunders so that I cannot hear what you say to the contrary." There is truth here. If what we are does not match what we say, it will be discounted. But to say that one Christian can be supportive to another merely by example is like saying that doctors can make people well by the evidence of their own health. It will not work. We have to learn the secret of health; we have to know the hindrances and the cure. So it is in support. People are drawn to the happy, useful life that is unselfish. Sin is audible, unbelief is vocal—they both advertise. Quiet influence will not win the world by support.

Support is also not intellectual. Great claims have been made for education by its sponsors, but we may as well face the fact that it does not make a person feel wanted. It doesn't take long before the observant student of life sees that while education makes strides every day in the training of minds in special subjects, it betrays a noticeable lack of power to train people to live life. It is possible to teach and even learn support and not be supportive.

Second, we must identify the areas of support that every Christian deeply needs and make those available in the small group setting. One great area of support that must be provided in this group environment is accountability. People need constant help. They want suggestions about how to study the Bible, where and what to read in it, when to pray, and how to pray.

Another area of support vital to the spiritual trek is fellowship. We can never get away from realizing that the health of our relationship to God will be partly dependent upon our integration in a guided group. The group's members live in close cooperation and fellowship with one another, sharing plans and needs, visions and sins, living in the light with one another. This is not a committee; it is not a party for mutual enjoyment. It is an opportunity to bounce off of other people the joys, pains, and discoveries that each one experiences.

Service

> Do all the good you can, by all the means you can, in all the ways you can, in all the places you can, at all the times you can, to all the people you can and as long as you can.—*John Wesley*[4]

The early church was filled with Christians who were instructed to contribute to the needs of the saints (Rom. 12:13) and show hospitality to strangers (Heb. 13:2). This early body of believers was practicing this life-style to such an extent that Luke was able to make this incredible observation: "For there was not a needy person among them" (Acts 4:34).

Our churches are filled with overweight Christians. No, not in a physical sense, but in light of spiritual intake. They sit and feed on Sunday morning. They snack during the Sunday School buffet. They listen to tapes during the week, read books, meet with others midweek to enjoy another supper. The church is getting overweight in knowledge and failing to provide a vehicle through which we Christians can demonstrate our love by meeting the needs of others and "working out our salvation." Small groups can provide a channel whereby members can embrace the philosophy of being on call to minister to one another. This small-group environment can and does create a resource bank of professional expertise, trade skills, and financial assistance.

So how is caring demonstrated in the small group? There are countless ways such as ministering to someone with material needs, or comforting someone who is facing the peril of some trial or agony, or even providing a place of counseling for those around us with spiritual problems. Expand your thinking! How about:

- Small-group members providing a new set of clothes for each child of a single parent.
- Small-group members doing the yard work monthly for a disabled person in the church.
- Small-group members taking on the responsibility to provide meals for families when one of their members is recovering from some debilitating disease or surgery.
- Small-group members making a car available for a missionary to use during furlough in the States.
- Small-group members taking on a special and necessary task at their church.

The list is endless and exciting, and you can be sure that the group will mature and bond in a way never experienced before when they get into the trenches together. These are ways of working out/off your spiritual intake and demonstrating the love of Jesus Christ in attractive ways to a burning-out society. We are called to be salt and light and to get outside of ourselves to make a difference.

Evaluation

Church growth studies have found that for a church to assimilate new people effectively it must have an average of seven small groups for every one hundred adult members. Take a few moments and list below all of the small groups available in your church.

To qualify as a small group a group must have the following three criteria.

1. It must be small—less than fifteen people.

2. It must meet on a regular basis—at least once per month.

3. It must create a sense of accountability—people will be missed if they are not there.

List of Small Groups

Transfer your list of small groups to figure 16 and identify the number of small groups still needed in your church.

Note below the church ministries which create, support, and train people in small groups. Then list what new ministries are needed.

Figure 16

Small Groups and a Can of Oil

A man was known to carry a little can of oil wherever he went. If he passed through a door that squeaked, he put a drop of oil on the hinges; if a gate was hard to open, he oiled the latch. He passed through life lubricating all the creaking places and making it a little more pleasant for those who followed after him.

Small groups are like that. They are settings for sharing, lubricating one another to be open and vulnerable. They are places of study where the squeaky hinges of discernment and understanding can run smoothly. They are places of support where we make sure each person carries an oil can and is looking for appropriate places to put a drop. Lastly, they are places to lubricate all the creaking places of our neighborhoods and relationships with the life-generating love of Jesus Christ.

The first-century church may be gone, but its principles are with us today.

> And day by day continuing with one mind in the temple, and breaking bread from house to house, they were taking their meals together with gladness and sincerity of heart, praising God, and having favor with all the people. And the Lord was adding to their number day by day those who were being saved. (Acts 2:46-47)

Notes

[1]Charles Spurgeon, quoted in *Sermons Illustrated* (Minneapolis: Jeff and Pam Carroll Publishers, 1989).

[2]Paul Lee Tan, *Encyclopedia of 7700 Illustrations* (Rockville, Md.: Assurance Publishers, 1979), 192.

[3]Ibid.

[4]Walter B. Knight, *Knight's Treasury of Illustrations* (Grand Rapids, Mich.: William B. Eerdmans, 1963), 357.

9
Assimilation Through Identification

As you fly over the North Atlantic Ocean you will see awesome icebergs floating in those cold and icy waters. If you look carefully, you will see a pattern develop: small icebergs move in one direction and gigantic icebergs move in another. The surface winds drive the small icebergs while the huge ones are controlled by the deep ocean currents.

There is a lesson in this for us. Lives are driven by two forces. "Small lives" are driven to and fro by the surface winds of change, petty problems, and disagreeable circumstances. Despair, depression, and discouragement overwhelm those "small lives." On the other hand, there are "great lives," gigantic in stature, which are never moved by the petty blowing of surface winds. These "giant lives," with foundations running deep in immovable faith, are controlled by the deep-running movements of a wise, loving, and all-powerful God. Let the winds blow! Let them move others around! Despite what happens, these lives remain steady and sure.

Just as there are the deeper currents that motivate us in our faith, there are also the deeper currents that motivate people to become assimilated into your church. They are drawn along by unseen factors which they identify with and support. This principle of identification includes three distinct areas of alignment necessary to the incorporation process.

Identification with the Purpose

Why are we here? What does God expect from the church? Is there any one given direction that we are to follow? These are the kinds of questions that people in today's churches are asking of themselves and of the leadership. Robert Dale calls this statement of purpose the "kingdom dream" in *To Dream Again*. He writes:

> A congregation's dream must be clearly known by its members. Yet a statement of a kingdom dream is rarely encompassed adequately by a few words. God's purpose of redemption is always greater than our imaginations, hopes, and vocabularies. But our continuing witness in word and life is our best vehicle for telling his story. Stating and publicizing your congregation's dream is critical. Either the sharp focus of your congregation's resources of people, facilities, money, energy, and information is on a defined dream or your church is using its resources ineffectively to some degree.[1]

The church needs direction. It is searching for the leadership to provide it with direction. The purpose statement of the church provides the biblical reasoning upon which this direction is formulated. Let's take some time to provide some guidelines for writing and helping people to identify with the purpose of the church.

First, establish a ministry area. A desire to "save" the world is a wonderful ideal, yet in all practicality improbable. Research has determined that the following is an accurate picture of the typical driving times for most church members.

> 20 percent drive 0-5 minutes
> 40 percent 5-15 minutes
> 23 percent drive 15-25 minutes

6 percent drive 25-35 minutes
5 percent drive 35-45 minutes
3 percent drive 45+ minutes[2]

A church's incorporation strategy must focus on those people within a three- to ten-mile radius. If people have to drive much farther than this, they will have trouble identifying with your church.

Second, establish a target audience. Whom do you hope to reach? What type of church are you building? If families are to be the focus, then the people need to hear the word *family* in the purpose. If the evangelism of the local community is the aim, make that clear. The purpose must provide a sense of direction by using words like *reach* and *teach.* Spend time evaluating the new residents, or people experiencing crisis, or the families with new babies. Establish your purpose based on their needs.

Third, condense this purpose into twenty-five words or less. This exercise causes the leadership to think through and prioritize the purpose. It makes the purpose easily memorized by the people. It becomes an opportunity for the pastor to spring-board into a complete series of messages on "The Direction of _____ Church," or "God's Purpose for _____ Church."

Fourth, make the purpose visible. Repetition is the key to learning. We must expose the people to outside experts who will validate and confirm the purpose. Seminars are appropriate. Consultants are extremely useful. Use a variety of media to convey the message. Slide shows, banners, newsletters, testimonies, prayers, and films can all be very effective. We must teach the purpose, especially to all the new members. The Pastor's Class or new-member orientation class is the best place to begin. Then, every Sunday School class must hear it, every leadership retreat must discuss it, and all planning must include it.

Fifth, the purpose and growth of the church must become a standing agenda item for staff and board meetings. Vital statistics must be gathered on attendance and Sunday School involvement. Critiques of curriculum and worship must be sought. Updates on follow up and visitation must be stressed. We all have our opinions, but facts are hard to argue against. Do not be afraid to ask for the presentation of charts and graphs to maintain a vivid perspective of the purpose and its fulfillment.

Identification with the Vision

If the purpose gives us the direction, then the vision provides us with the motivation for accomplishing the purpose.

There is a fear that permeates churches throughout our land, a fear based upon a warped view of church growth and God's vision for His church. For any church to have an active assimilation program, these misconceptions must be silenced, or the church will continue to stagnate and maintain instead of growing. Let us look at three major misunderstandings that we must correct before we can provide a means whereby the people in our churches can identify with the vision.

Large Is Not Lethal

On the Day of Pentecost, the early church in Jerusalem, made up of 120 members, added 3,000 to its fellowship. That's a 2,600 percent increase in membership! Those new members reached out into the urban community around them, gaining favor with other people. And day after day the Lord added to their numbers.

Quality and quantity were merely two aspects of the

same reality. Evangelistic effectiveness was a *quality* measured in *quantitative* terms. Follow through the Book of Acts and see dynamic church growth. Large was not lethal; it was the vision to reach out to more and more unsaved. We saw the early church grow from a small band of 120 disciples to 3,000 more believers on the Day of Pentecost. But do not stop there. In Acts 4:4 we read, "But many of them who had heard the word believed; and the number of the men [was] about five thousand." With careful detail, Luke recorded the growth pattern since Pentecost. The membership of the Jerusalem church then stood at 5,000. The church was growing.

As we come to Acts 5:14, we see a change in emphasis as Luke wrote, "And believers were the more added to the Lord, multitudes both of men and women" (KJV). Here the emphasis is upon the fact that there were *multitudes* of men and women added. Notice the change in attention to multiplication instead of addition. We can be certain that this was a growing church.

Any church that makes a decision not to embrace this truth fails to realize the priorities outlined in the Scriptures. Large is not lethal. It is the outcome of a church realizing the Great Commission and structuring its vision to work toward it.

Evangelism Is Not Inclusion

People need to belong. It is possible for our churches to be evangelistic, yet cold and exclusive in their fellowship. Don't get me wrong. People need to be reached, baptized, and taught sound doctrine. But can all of this happen while people sense exclusion from the internal fellowship of the church? This is why small-group ministry discussed in the previous chapter is so vital. Many churches with whom I have consulted and worked portray a virile desire to reach the lost. Yet, just as people walk in the front door, so too, they can exit via the back door. Church growth statistics have demonstrated that new members must identify with the church. If they don't establish relationships and a sense of belonging, they'll stop attending or go elsewhere.

The problem with finding ways to include people is the incredible complexity of social schemes in our society. We see the need for singles ministries, ministries to the divorced, single-parent ministries, abuse recovery—the list goes on and on. Smaller churches tend to isolate themselves from these "fringe" personalities. This doesn't happen consciously. These kinds of people do not feel welcome, so they do not stay. However, we are convinced that inclusion is the main ingredient to identification.

Lyle Schaller illustrates this principle by two concentric circles.

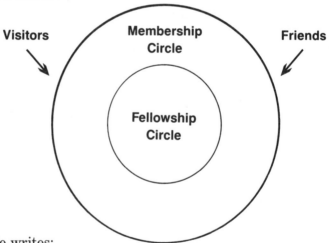

He writes:

> From the perspective of the leaders, the long-time members and heritage-oriented people inside that

inner circle, the line marking the boundary of the fellowship circle is no higher than the line painted on a gymnasium floor. Anyone who is interested and willing to take the initiative can step across it very easily and become a part of that inner circle. Some of the members of that inner circle go one step further and insist either that the line does not exist or that it is actually coterminous with the outer membership boundary.

A radically different picture is perceived, however, by the members who are outside that fellowship circle. Instead of a thin line painted on the floor, many of them perceive the boundary of that fellowship circle to be a circular masonry wall six feet thick and thirty feet high. They see a high, thick, and forbidding wall with several doors in it.[3]

He concludes that assimilation transcends heritage and traditional loyalty but involves an identification with the people's dreams. Inclusion is much more than evangelism.

Needs Are More Than Knowledge

Education is a vital ingredient to an effective church program. Unfortunately, there have been some who are proponents of the notion that people will join a church solely upon its ability to "feed" them. Have you not also heard people say that they left a church because they were not being fed?

Today's church climate is much more complex than this simplistic attitude. We need to balance "reach out and teach" with a "reach out and touch" attitude. Relationships do not develop through education and knowledge. They develop as our churches identify with the needs of people.

Society seems to be falling apart around us. Marriages are on the rocks; the suicide rate of teens is on the increase; and sexual immorality appears to be a norm. Where can people turn for the "experience" of Christ's love? Where are people going to "experience" acceptance and care? The education system or the local church?

Specialists in the area of church dynamics and church growth contend that 75 to 90 percent of all the people in today's churches are there because a friend or relative invited them. We have already seen that people need to develop friendships within the first six to twelve months of attendance. One need not be a paid consultant to see that people in search of a church yearn for relationships.

Teaching deserves more of our attention. It is a great way to promote spiritual growth and endurance as we will study in detail in the following chapter. But teaching ministries must blend with the "need" ministries of the body. One church in Southern California that I worked with extensively for three years established a task force to enable it to check up on new members and to follow up on their continued success. That's a great idea. Lay-shepherding programs, pastoral care staff, and visitation ministries all provide ample means of touching people where they need, not where they know.

Scripture explains that "[without a] vision, the people perish" (Prov. 29:18, KJV). But I want to tell you that with a vision, the people in your church will not only tackle the impossible, but accomplish it. I heard a story about a gang of laborers digging a hole five feet square by ten feet deep. After grueling hours of hard labor, they finally got the hole dug. The boss had never bothered to tell them the purpose for digging the hole. In fact, after they had finished their task, even before they could glow in their accomplishment, they were told to fill in the hole.

Immediately, the men walked off the job and said, "We

quit, we want our pay now!" When the boss asked why, they replied, "Digging holes and filling them up only makes fools of us." Then the boss took the time to explain that there was a distinct purpose for his request. A leaking gas line in the vicinity was endangering the lives of the community. Once they found out there was a purpose in their digging, not only did they stay on the job, but they also identified with the vision.

Every man and woman who comes to your church wants his or her life to count, and a vision will give meaning and purpose service. People will come to your church to look. They will not stay out of duty, they will stay because the enthusiasm of a vision has caught their hearts, and they have been swept up in the desire to thrive, not only survive.

Identification with the Great Commission

The cockpit of a plane is filled with a myriad of gauges and dials. The altimeter gauge enables you to determine your elevation and rate of climb and descent. A fuel gauge is vital for the pilot's calculations of distance and range of travel. One gauge primary to the well-being and ease of flight of the pilot is the attitude gauge. The performance of the plane depends upon its attitude. Changing the attitude changes the aircraft's overall performance. The pilot need only bring the airplane into a nose-high attitude in order to climb and slow down. Bringing the plane into a nose-down attitude causes the vehicle to dive and speed up. This is what some pilots have called "attitude flying."

Leading a church takes an attitude adjustment. Win Arn speaks of the church today in need of a "Great Commission Conscience." In his *Basic Church Growth Seminar* he shares:

It is an *attitude* which permeates the thinking and decision-making process of a church. It is an *attitude* which sees people outside of Christ as lost. It is an *attitude* which resonates with the Great Commission found in its various forms throughout Scripture. It is an *attitude* which sees missions as both "over there" and "right here." It is an *attitude* which motivates both corporate and personal action in prayer, giving and service for Great Commission results.[4]

Arn suggests ten self-evaluating statements that can enable the church, its leadership, and each individual to evaluate their attitudes toward the Great Commission. How many of the following questions can you answer with a "yes"?

1. I see the primary purpose of the church as responding to the Great Commission.

2. I have participated in an outreach/training event in the last year.

3. I have invited an unchurched friend/relative to a church event in the last six months.

4. I would support a motion to designate at least ten percent of our budget to outreach events/training/activities to reach our own community with the gospel.

5. I would prefer that the pastor call on non-members more often than members.

6. I would be willing to take a new member/visitor home for dinner at least once every six months.

7. I have intentionally introduced myself to a new member or visitor in the past month.

8. I have talked to an unchurched person about my faith in the past six months.

9. I have prayed for a specific unchurched person in the past month.

10. I would be willing to be the pioneer in a new group or new church fellowship to help reach the new people.

A score of seven or more is a great indication of a "nose-high" attitude for the direction of your life and/or church. And remember—if there is a nose-low attitude, descent is rapid.

Evaluation

Effective churches have specific ministries designed to help people identify with their purpose, vision, and commission. Briefly list the ministries of your church which are specifically designed to help people identify with your body.

Ministries of Identification

Transfer these ministries to figure 17 and list the number of identification ministries still needed.

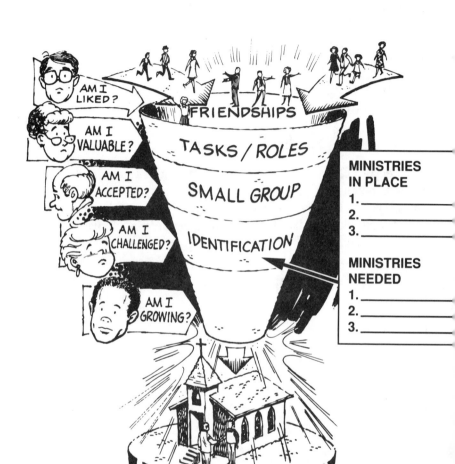

Figure 17

On a cold Sunday morning in Chicago with the wind chill factor fifteen below zero, a little orphan boy walked four miles to church. An older man met him at the door, shook his hand, and greeted him with his usual smile. "Glad to see you; sure is cold today," the older man said. The young boy smiled back and shared that he had walked four long miles in that cold. Surprised, the older man inquired, "You mean that you walked in this cold wind to church this morning?"

The boy replied, "I didn't have the bus fare."

The old man was a little stumped and asked, "How many churches did you pass along the way?"

"Sixteen," was the boy's answer. "Sixteen."

"So why did you walk such a long way to come here today?"

The boy didn't hesitate and, as he took off his wooly jacket, told the man, "Because this is my church."

Young and old, people will go to the church where they identify, where the deeper currents of their faith continue to move and the deeper currents of their relationships continue to be met.

Notes

[1]Robert Dale, *To Dream Again* (Nashville: Broadman Press, 1981), 44-45.

[2]Win Arn, *The Win Arn Growth Report,* No. 20 (Monrovia, Calif.: Church Growth Press), 1-4.

[3]Lyle Schaller, *Assimilating New Members* (Nashville: Abingdon Press, 1978), 81.

[4]Win Arn, *Basic Church Growth Seminar* (Monrovia, Calif.: Church Growth Press, 1985), 17.

10
Assimilation Through Spiritual Growth

Not long before Henry Wadsworth Longfellow's death at age seventy-five, someone asked him how he continued to write so beautifully and remain so vigorous. Longfellow pointed to an apple tree that was full of colorful blooms and said,

> That is a very old apple tree, but the blossoms this year seem more beautiful than ever before. That old tree grows a little new wood each year, and I suppose it is out of the new wood that these blossoms come. Like the apple tree, I try to grow a little new wood each year.

You and I need to grow a little new wood every year whether we have been in church two weeks, two months, or twenty years. Spiritual growth is an often overlooked facet of the incorporation strategy, but necessary and vital. Our present-day mind-set is one that wants nurture and challenge, and when we do not receive it, we move on to a new environment.

Leading a church presents us with all kinds of new challenges based upon changes in our world during the past thirty or forty years. We have seen incredible changes in church commitment. In the 1950s, people joined a church for life. Today people are "graduating" to the bigger churches after a two- to three-year stay in a smaller church. In the 1950s, there was social pressure to attend church. Today, we see social competition to keep people from church. The divorce rate is four times greater than in the 1950s. The percentage of couples living together is ten times greater than in 1975. Our world is in a state of flux, and in the middle of this rapidly declining and rapidly degenerating environment, we find the typical church steeped in 1950s tradition. The churches are filled with 1990s families wanting to grow and mature in their faith but experiencing disillusionment and frustration.

There are "four deadly signs" that inhibit spiritual growth: isolation, fragmentation, stagnation, and confrontation. We call these root-severing problems "signs" because they can be used to understand why a person may be dropping out. Each of these signs is worthy of a closer examination.

Isolation

God has a master plan for His church.

> I, therefore, the prisoner of the Lord, entreat you to walk in a manner worthy of the calling with which you have been called, with all humility and gentleness, with patience, showing forbearance to one another in love, being diligent to preserve the unity of the Spirit in the bond of peace. There is one body and one Spirit, just as also you are called in one hope of your calling; one Lord, one faith, one baptism, one God and Father of all who is over all and through all and in all. (Eph. 4:1-6)

You and I may be like the guide who was hired by some hunters to take them into the backwoods of Maine. After some days, they became hopelessly lost and quite naturally began to doubt the competence of their guide. "You said you were the best guide in Maine," they reminded him.

"I am," he said, "but I think we are in Canada now."[1]

It is easy for people to become lost or feel isolated. Theological changes or emotional choices can cause us to wander in a foreign land apart from the fellowship we so desire and possibly stray from the will of God. Each of us carries a self portrait inside, a picture created using the brush of life and touched up day after day. Each stroke of the brush, as small as it may appear, will contribute to a finished canvas later in life. People who carry around a picture that is a little out of focus or distorted by painful memories will tend to isolate themselves for protection.

Life is no longer simple. Today's technologies have created a new wave of expectations and pressures. It was not long ago when life's issues revolved around existence—whether or not there was a roof over our heads or food on the table. In the Western world we have become preoccupied with the quality of our lives. We are an affluent society caught on an ever-quickening treadmill that insists that our lives must always be getting bigger and better. We are bent on success and when we do not achieve it we fall into an isolation mode.

Success is more than achievement. People want to be more important than things. When we begin to think in terms of the kingdom, we can overcome the dehumanization of the world. Henry David Thoreau, the American essayist, put it well: "Why should we be in such desperate haste to succeed, and in such desperate enterprises? If a man does not keep pace with his companions, perhaps it's because he hears a different drummer. Let him step to the music which he hears, however measured or far away."

Fragmentation

Disunity is a lot like cancer. One surgeon describes the similarity this way:

> A tumor is called benign if its effect is fairly local-ized and it stays within membrane boundaries. But the most traumatizing condition in the body occurs when disloyal cells defy inhibition. They multiply without any checks on growth, spreading rapidly throughout the body, choking out normal cells. White cells, armed against foreign invaders, will not attack the body's own mutinous cells. Phy-sicians fear no other malfunction more deeply; it is called cancer. For still mysterious reasons, these cells—and they may be tissues—grow wild, out of control. Each is a healthy functioning cell, but dis-loyal, no longer acting in regard for the rest of the body.[2]

Tragically, this is an accurate description of breakdown both in the human and spiritual body.

God's design is to have the church "fitly joined to-gether" (Eph. 4:16, KJV), but Satan's design is to disrupt all attempts at ministry and spreading the good news of salvation. Disunity, whether it be in a group or individu-ally, is a reality. It leaves in its wake broken lives and people who are discouraged and painfully hurt. This pain has caused many in the body of Christ to become apathetic toward the new life that they could be enjoying. As I have had the privilege of working with many pas-tors and lay leaders, I hear over and over how this fragmentation has obliterated any sense of the presence of God's love in individuals and faith in the overall com-munity of the church.

Fragmentation has some very obvious characteristics. An alert individual can perceive fragmentation and work through it if he watches for indicator lights.

Step one: The cooling stage. People wear their emotions on their sleeves, and their actions are seen as a little cold or reluctant.

Step two: The concern stage. Letters are mailed to the pastor or key leaders expressing their disappointments and concerns.

Step three: The meddlesome stage. Nit-picking questions begin to surface. "Are we meeting the budget?" "Why do we need to change?" Disunity is now beginning to mobilize.

Step four: The resistance stage. The people will now either ridicule the leadership or retreat from all involvement. Accusations are made, sides are drawn, and fragmentation occurs.

Stagnation

Between an airplane and every other form of locomotion and transportation there is one great contrast. The horse and wagon, the automobile, the bicycle, the locomotive, the speedboat, and the great battleship—all can come to a standstill without danger, and they can all reverse their engines, or their power, and go back.

But there is no reverse about the engine of an airplane. It cannot back up. It dare not stand still. If it loses its momentum and forward drive, then it crashes. The only safety for the airplane is in its forward and upward motion. The only safe direction for the Christian to take is forward and upward. If he stops, or if he begins to slip and go backward, that moment he is in danger.[3]

How many Christians do we find today who have stopped growing in their faith? The Scriptures are filled with commands to maintain activity and continued growth. "For you were formerly darkness, but now you are light in the Lord; walk as children of light" (Eph.

5:8). "I urge you therefore, brethren, by the mercies of God, to present your bodies a living and holy sacrifice, acceptable to God, which is your spiritual service of worship" (Rom. 12:1). "Brethren, I do not regard myself as having laid hold of it yet; but one thing I do: forgetting what lies behind and reaching forward to what lies ahead, I press on toward the goal for the prize of the upward call of God in Christ Jesus" (Phil. 3:13-14). We never find in the Word of God a call to sit back, take a year off, and stop maturing.

So why are people leaving the church as a result of a loss of zeal and desire to study and serve? The answer is found when we examine the world in which we live. Social scientists have identified three distinct ages which serve as a brief outline of history. First, there was the "agriculture age,"[4] a period of time ending in the mid-1800s. During these years, 90 percent of all work revolved around farming and the small rural town was the premier focus. Then from the mid-1800s to the mid-1900s, we saw an explosion of industrialization. The "industrial age"[5] began the growth of cities and factories, and expansion was on everyone's mind. But, from the mid-1900s until today, we are in an age of technology, an "information age." Computers are now a part of the typical learning environment. Over 9,600 different periodicals are published in the United States each year. Newsstands offer a choice of 2,500 different magazines. We have the yellow pages, telemarketing, extensive libraries, and educational videos. We are in information overload.

We have found many implications worthy of our examination brought on by this information thrust. All these implications are influencing our churches today.

Travel: In 1911, the typical American averaged 2,640 miles per year in travel. Today, the average car owner averages 10,000 miles per year with some traveling 30,000 or more miles per year! Many people will travel over 3,000,000 miles in their lifetimes.

Implication: People are tired, have less free time, and are more difficult to recruit.

Change: The world today is as different from fifty years ago as 1940 was from the time of Julius Caesar. Within a couple of decades, the share of the industrialized nations' work force engaged in manufacturing will be no more than 5 percent to 10 percent. "Knowledge workers" will take their place.

Implication: People oppose change, resist making friends, and wonder why they are lonely.

Saturation: In one year the average American will read or complete three thousand notices and forms, read 100 newspapers and 36 magazines, watch 2,463 hours of television, listen to 730 hours of radio, buy 20 records, talk on the telephone almost 61 hours, and read 3 books.

Implication: People hear so much noise, so much "informational cacophony," that they are not going to hear you.

Specialization: The sheer volume of data makes it inevitable that we must focus on the narrow endeavor. Our information explosion results in a fragmentation of knowledge leading to specialization, overspecialization, and subspecialization.

Implication: People cannot see the big picture, tie the ends together, or see how the pieces relate.

Memory: People are plagued with "Chinese-dinner" memory dysfunction! They forget what they learn within one hour! This problem is created by placing an emphasis on short-term memory characterized by cramming unnecessary information for unnecessary tests to get unnecessary grades.

Implication: People hear information, learn it, and lose it without much effect on their lives.

Inaccuracies: The General Accounting Office of the IRS found when the IRS received tax questions by mail, 53 percent were answered correctly, 31 percent contained major errors, and 16 percent were unclear or incomplete. When the IRS received phone calls, 36 percent of the callers were given wrong answers!

Implication: People know information is out there, have difficulty getting it, and make mistakes without it.

Amnesia: Overload amnesia results when the brain shuts down to protect itself. You cannot recall even simple information such as a friend's name when trying to introduce her to another person. This often happens in classrooms, conferences, lectures, and while attending church.

Implication: People hear more than they understand, forget what they already know, and resist learning more.

Confusion: Everyone knows the feeling of buying a high-technology product (like a VCR), getting it home, and not understanding how to use it. Each new form the IRS adds for income tax preparation reportedly adds an additional twenty minutes of time for completion.

Implication: People don't know how to use what they learn, make mistakes when they try, and feel guilty about it.[6]

Do you see our problem? We have so much information, so much data, that we are no longer challenged to personal growth—we wait to be programmed. We begin to hear statements like "I'm no longer getting anything out of the pastor's messages" or "When are we going to study something that I'll enjoy?" Assimilation for these people will lose all of its effectiveness when knowledge is our focus; relationships must come to the forefront. Any incorporation strategy that is not keenly aware of those caught in strictly an information mode will lack influence in the church. There will only be stagnation when there is no running water, when there is no forward direction. The problem in this forward progression is never found in a handout or directive reading.

Confrontation

"Confrontation is part of the Christian life, expect it!" Those were the words of a dear pastor who was having difficulty in his church. Yet when he shared that thought, he displayed much of today's attitude about confrontation, that it is a bad, unhealthy event. Is that always true? Can there be good and healthy confrontation?

Confrontation, in regard to an assimilation strategy, occurs in three different settings. First, we have the undefined expectations of the church. Any time a church or any organization does not have a clear purpose statement and a clear focus, there will be confrontation. People want direction; they desire to be led. Effective assimilation must include defined expectations so that the body can be unified in its vision.

Second, we often see unexpected conflicts in the body. Here we do not have a problem with vision, we have a problem with sin and sin will always lead to confrontation. It may be personal confrontation where the Holy Spirit convicts a person of the need to repent. It can be corporate confrontation in which a fragmented group is not happy with the direction of the church or changes that are being made. It is even sometimes authoritative conflict where a person may be having difficulty with the leadership. Whatever made the conflict, confrontation is the result.

Then last, we often hear the unannounced proposals from the leadership. Here the problem is communication. People want to know what is going on; they long to be included. Many of the conflicts that long-standing members will have come when the newly assimilated members take on positions of leadership and responsibility, and the "older" members feel neglected or not needed. Their confrontation is the result of anticipated changes due to "those new people." Open channels of communication are vital for the well being of a flock; they are the essence of all assimilation strategies.

Understanding the "Four Deadly Signs"

Now that we have a basic understanding of these four deadlies, let's try to relate them to Longfellow's tree and growth.

Our Lord often used the analogy of growth with an understanding of nature's biological needs. In John 15 we read:

> I am the true vine, and My Father is the vine-dresser. Every branch in Me that does not bear fruit, He takes away; and every branch that bears fruit, He prunes it, that it may bear more fruit. Abide in Me, and I in you. As the branch cannot bear fruit of itself, unless it abides in the vine, so neither can you, unless you abide in Me. I am the vine, you are the branches; he who abides in Me, and I in him, he bears much fruit; for apart from Me you can do nothing. (vv. 1-2,4-5)

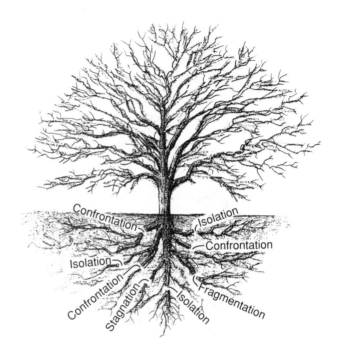

Figure 18[7]

Here lies the problem. Much of the nurturing that can be ours is not happening because the roots have been severed by the deadlies (see fig. 18). God has not abandoned the church. We are the ones who have left, cutting ourselves off from the source of life. When there is not a constant flow of the Holy Spirit's nutrients into our lives, we will not grow. There must be a healing, and this healing for effective incorporation to occur is not an automatic process. After we understand the four deadly signs—isolation, fragmentation, stagnation, and confrontation—it then becomes our task to draw people back into the body. This is assimilation (see fig. 19).

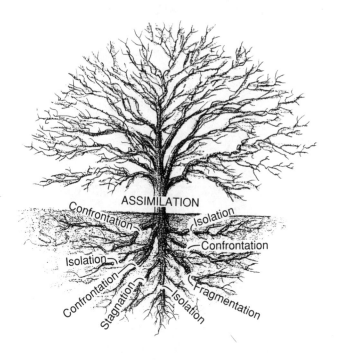

Figure 19[8]

As the church begins to eliminate the barriers of fragmentation, the walls of isolation, the pain of confrontation, and even the laziness of stagnation, new life will begin to flow through the roots of their soul and begin to rejuvenate the spiritual life of the person as a whole. They will sense a greater degree of identification with Christ and a renewed desire to reconcile with others (see fig. 20).

But we can never stop there, because the strong winds of trials and problems will always be waging war within our assemblies. Struggles are never far away. So effective incorporation goes a step further to provide the necessary ties that will anchor this person when the winds once again blow (see fig. 21).

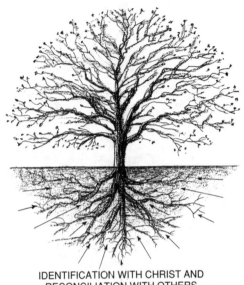

IDENTIFICATION WITH CHRIST AND
RECONCILIATION WITH OTHERS

Figure 20[9]

Spiritual counsel may be necessary for the person or family to get back on track. Your elders and deacons will find it necessary to monitor each person's involvement in the small-group setting, as friendships will be crucial. The church must seek to make those who are struggling feel exceptionally welcomed and wanted. Even the person's place of employment must be prayed for and supported. Then, and only then, will he or she again be open for what occurs when God's people come together: the challenging, feeding, pruning, encouraging, and instruction (see fig. 22).

In Colossians 2:6-7 we have the outcome of this kind of effective assimilation: "As you therefore have received Christ Jesus the Lord, so walk in Him, having been firmly rooted and now being built up in Him and established in your faith, just as you were instructed, and overflowing with gratitude."

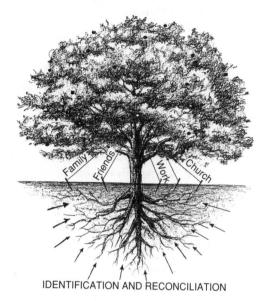

IDENTIFICATION AND RECONCILIATION

Figure 21[10]

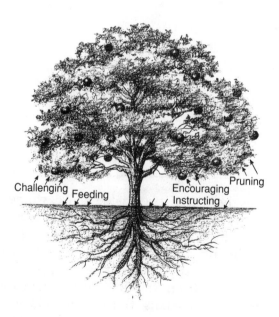

Figure 22[11]

Evaluation

Effective churches have specific ministries designed to help people break down the walls of confrontation, isolation, stagnation, and fragmentation. These ministries make the people accountable to one another and urge the people to continue to move forward in their growth. Briefly list below those ministries in your church which aid in the breakdown of these barriers to spiritual growth, realizing that some of these will obviously overlap with other areas.

Ministries of Spiritual Growth

Transfer those ministries listed above, whose responsibility is the maturation of your church attenders, to figure 23 and identify ministries that need to be added.

During his illustrious career, Babe Ruth, one of the greatest hitters in the history of baseball, hit 714 home runs. He is not only an American hero, but also a legend to us who are sports fans. But in Babe's long baseball career, he was not always on top of the world. In one of his

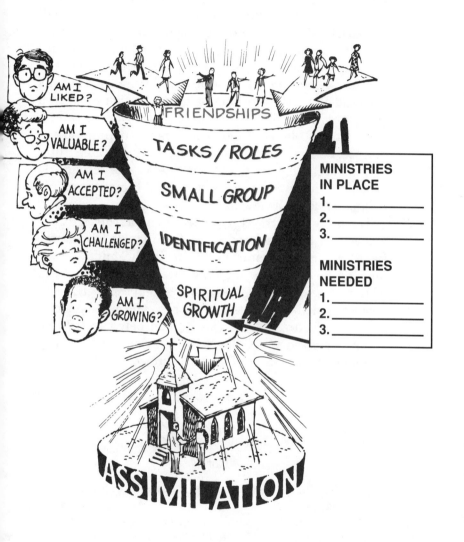

Figure 23

last full major league games, he played very poorly. The Braves played the Reds in Cincinnati. Age had caught up with the Babe, and he was no longer the agile runner and strong arm. During the game, he bobbled the ball and threw badly. In one inning alone, his errors were responsible for most of the five runs scored by Cincinnati.

As Babe walked off the field after that game and headed for the dugout, the booing of the fans reached his ears and cut to the quick of his heart. At that moment a young boy who idolized the hero jumped over the railing and onto the playing field. With tears streaming down his face, he threw his arms around the legs of Babe Ruth.

The baseball great didn't hesitate for one second. He picked up the boy, hugged him, and set him down on his feet, patting his head gently.

The noise from the stands came to an abrupt halt. No longer was Babe isolated from the fans. No longer was Babe facing confrontation. There in the midst of the hush of the crowd, the fans saw two heroes: Babe Ruth, who in spite of a dismal day on the field could still care about a little boy; and the small boy, who cared enough about the feelings of another human being to try and break down the walls. Together, the Babe and the boy had melted the hearts of a hostile crowd.

Notes

[1]Bruce Larson, *A Call to Holy Living* (Minneapolis: Augsburg Press, 1988). 21.

[2]Paul E. Brand and Philip Yancey, *Fearfully and Wonderfully Made* (Grand Rapids: Zondervan Publishing House, 1980), 59.

[3]Paul Lee Tan, *Encyclopedia of 7700 Illustrations* (Rockville, Md.: Assurance Publishers, 1979), 182-84.

[4]Toffler, Alvin, *The Third Wave* (New York: Bantam Books, 1980), 4.

[5]Ibid., 68.

[6]Gary McIntosh, *Church Growth Network* (San Bernardino, Calif., August 1989), 1-2.

[7]Adapted from Neil T. Anderson, *Spiritual Conflicts and Biblical Counseling* (La Habra, Calif.: Freedom in Christ Ministries, 1990), 45. Used by permission.

[8]Ibid., 46.

[9]Ibid., 47.

[10]Ibid., 48.

[11]Ibid., 50.

Evaluation
Develop Your Assimilation Strategy

A clergyman once remarked to Sir John Barbirolli how he wished he could fill his church building the way Sir John and the Halle Orchestra filled every seat of a large concert hall. The conductor replied, "You could, if you had a hundred members who worked together as well as the members of this orchestra."

Have you ever seen a performance of a symphony orchestra? I say "seen" because the harmony of the musicians is clearly visible. The white cuffs of the violinists stand out against a black background and make a bold horizontal line across the left side of the stage. As they play, those white cuffs remain an almost perfectly straight line which often moves up and down very quickly. It is a splendid demonstration of how the members of a great orchestra not only play the right notes but play them together.

A great church is somewhat like a great orchestra. The members will not only make the right moves but will make them together. The members must learn to decide upon a task and execute it with perfect harmony. A musician who always wants to play a favorite piece (which may be exceptionally beautiful) and refuses to play, or else plays very half-heartedly or slowly when another composition is chosen, will hurt the whole orchestra and may destroy its appeal. And a church member who is out of step with others, and who approaches tasks carelessly or reluctantly, may generate more sour music than the sweet notes that all the rest can draw out.

Review your Assimilation Strategy

New people to your church come with a number of questions on their minds. As they drive into the church parking lot, they wonder if they will easily find a place to park. Entering the front door, they wonder if they will be warmly welcomed. Sitting in the auditorium, they wonder if they will be embarrassed.

However, they have more crucial questions than these on their minds that your church must answer in a positive way if they are to assimilate into your church. Am I liked? Am I valuable? Am I accepted? Am I challenged? Am I growing?

These questions illustrate the assimilation process that people follow entering your church. Take the following quiz to evaluate how well your church answers these questions.

1. Our church has an effective way to welcome people which does not embarrass them.   YES   NO

2. Our church has entry level places of service available to new people.   YES   NO

3. Our church has an average of seven small groups for every one hundred adults.   YES   NO

4. Our church has a purpose statement of twenty-five words or less that people have memorized.   YES   NO

5. Our church has a Christian education curriculum which meets the felt needs of the congregation.   YES   NO

6. Our church has regular socials especially to help new members make friends.   YES   NO

7. Our church has a way to help new people discover and use their gifts.   YES   NO

8. Our church has started at least two new groups in the last year.   YES   NO

9. Our church has a vision for the future which people understand and are challenged by.   YES   NO

10. Our church has a worship service which equips people to meet the real issues of their lives.   YES   NO

11. Our church people can identify a minimum of seven friends in our church.   YES   NO

12. Our church has an involvement level of at least 60 percent.   YES   NO

13. Our church has a variety of small groups available.   YES   NO

14. Our church has a strong Great Commission conscience.   YES   NO

15. Our people sense that they are growing spiritually.   YES   NO

Tally your answers below by checking the box beside each question answered YES above. Then add up the checked boxes across and place the number of checked boxes on the line at the right of each series.

Questions			Total	Strategy
1 ☐	6 ☐	11 ☐	___	Friendships
2 ☐	7 ☐	12 ☐	___	Roles/Tasks
3 ☐	8 ☐	13 ☐	___	Small Groups
4 ☐	9 ☐	14 ☐	___	Identification
5 ☐	10 ☐	15 ☐	___	Spiritual Growth

Grand Total ___

1- 5 points = Poor: Overall unbalanced strategy

6-10 points = Good: Strong in some areas, weak in others

11-15 points = Excellent: Overall balanced strategy

Develop Your Assimilation Strategy

You completed the funnel model as you have been reading each of the last five chapters. Now, take a moment to transfer your findings from figures 14, 15, 16, 17, and 23 to figure 24. Take a close look at your overall assimilation strategy. Where is it strong and where is it weak?

Again, I want to remind you that your strategy is strong if you have three ministries listed in each of the five areas. Your strategy is good if there are two listed for each area and poor if each area has only one or no ministries listed. Remember, your assimilation strategy can be strong in one or two areas and weak in the others. For example, you might have three ministries under friendship and task/roles, but almost none under the remaining three. Not only will there be a "bottle-neck" in the funnel leading to assimilation, but also your assimilation strategy will be out of balance.

KEEPING THEM – EVALUATING YOUR CHURCH

	MINISTRIES IN PLACE	MINISTRIES NEEDED	MINISTRIES PLANNED
FRIENDSHIPS	1. 2. 3.	1. 2. 3.	1. 2. 3.
TASKS / ROLES	1. 2. 3.	1. 2. 3.	1. 2. 3.
SMALL GROUP	1. 2. 3.	1. 2. 3.	1. 2. 3.
IDENTIFICATION	1. 2. 3.	1. 2. 3.	1. 2. 3.
SPIRITUAL GROWTH	1. 2. 3.	1. 2. 3.	1. 2. 3.

Take a moment to review your completed model. In the box below, briefly describe your church's overall assimilation strategy. Where are your strengths? Where are your weaknesses?

Overall Assimilation Strategy

Well, how did you do? I have tried to help you with those in-between steps where we can refocus where we are in relation to the world and the will of God.

Jackie Gleason told a story of a man who rode his little blue bicycle through a customs checkpoint. Every day at the same time, he rode up. Every time his bicycle basket held three jars: one filled with sand, one filled with water, and one filled with nuts and bolts. The customs agents were suspicious that this man was smuggling, so they would often open up the jars—but the sand was just sand, the water was just water, the nuts and bolts were just nuts and bolts. Sometimes they would frisk the man, and on a few occasions they even took the bicycle apart. No contraband was ever found. Yet since this man came through their checkpoint every single day, and no one ever saw him riding back, they just knew he had to be smuggling something.

Several years later, one of the customs agents stopped the man on the little blue bicycle and said: "Today is my last day. I'm going to retire. I have no desire to catch you, but for the sake of my peace of mind, could you tell me what you've been smuggling all these years?"

The man replied, "I've been smuggling little blue bicycles."

The moral of the story is simple. For our sacred concerns, sometimes the answer is the one that's obvious and unconcealed. Many of the strategies needed in your church have become much clearer. Now begin taking steps to plan effective strategies to find new people and keep them.

Are you ready? Head forward, stop; head back, stop. Don't laugh—that's how it goes!

*About
the
Authors*

Gary McIntosh is associate professor of Practical Theology and director of the D.Min. Program at the Talbot School of Theology. He is a graduate of Fuller Theological Seminary (D.Min.), Western Conservative Baptist Seminary (M.Div.), and Rockmont College (B.A.). He is a member of the North American Society of Church Growth and editor of the *Church Growth Network Newsletter*. He and his wife, Carol, have two sons, Gary and Aaron.

Glen Martin is senior pastor of Community Baptist Church in Manhattan Beach, California. He is a graduate of the Talbot School of Theology (D.Min. and M.Div.) and the University of LaVerne (B.A.). Glen is a member of the North American Society of Church Growth and a consultant for the Church Growth Network. He and his wife have one daughter, Kerry, and two sons, Scott and David.